Meeting SEN
in the Curriculum:
ICT

Other titles in the Meeting Special Needs in the Curriculum series:

Meeting Special Needs in English
Tim Hurst
1 84312 157 3

Meeting Special Needs in Maths
Brian Sharp
1 84312 158 1

Meeting Special Needs in Citizenship
Alan Combes
1 84312 169 7

Meeting Special Needs in Religious Education
Dilwyn Hunt
1 84312 167 0

Meeting Special Needs in History
Richard Harris and Ian Luff
1 84312 163 8

Meeting Special Needs in Design and Technology
Louise Davies
1 84312 166 2

Meeting Special Needs in Art
Kim Earle and Gill Curry
1 84312 161 1

Meeting Special Needs in Music
Victoria Jacquiss and Diane Paterson
1 84312 168 9

Meeting Special Needs in Modern Foreign Languages
Sally McKeown
1 84312 165 4

Meeting Special Needs in Science
Carol Holden
1 84312 159 X

Meeting Special Needs in Geography
Diane Swift
1 84312 162 X

Meeting Special Needs in PE and Sport
Crispin Andrews
1 84312 164 6

Contents

Foreword

'I want every child, every young person, every learner, wherever they are, to achieve their full potential. ICT has an important place in making that possible. By aiding teaching and learning. By opening up new ways to learn and new places to learn in. By extending choice. By allowing greater tailoring to the individual.'

Ruth Kelly, Secretary of State for Education & Skills
BETT 2005, Keynote Address

Technology has the ability to make teachers better teachers and to make their jobs easier. It brings a wealth of resources, offers opportunities to support different learning styles, and makes the learning environment accessible, stimulating and rewarding. ICT is also a subject in its own right and one in which pupils with special educational needs can excel if given appropriate opportunities and effective support. The authors of this book have pooled their extensive experience to present invaluable guidance to teachers and teacher assistants who want to create those opportunities and provide the best support.

Looking around classrooms today, exciting and innovative use of technology is part of an overall approach to teaching – making the idea of a curriculum for all very real. ICT can remove barriers to achievement, enable teachers to set ever higher standards and empower learners to fulfil their ambitions.

We still have some way to go when using ICT with pupils with SEN. There is always a danger that the cleverness of the technology leads people to believe that ICT itself will solve a learner's difficulties or meet their needs. It will not. It is the way teachers use that technology and how they integrate it with their teaching and learning that unlocks the power of the technology to support students. We talk, for example, about 'interactive' whiteboards and the opportunities they give for pupils to learn actively and access multi-sensory learning. However, the real power of a whiteboard is as a tool in the hands of a skilled teacher who is engaging a pupil, group or class in active learning.

This book explores all these points and informs teachers about the ways in which technology can help them to meet the many demands placed on them today. It also explores ways in which technology can be fully integrated with the everyday tools teachers use to make learning exciting – and to deliver that full and balanced curriculum which is the entitlement of every pupil.

Chris Stevens
Head of Inclusion
Learning and Teaching Directorate
Becta

Acknowledgements

The authors would like to thank:

Sue Stevens, Information and Communication Technology Consultants (ICTC)
Maggie Wagstaff, Warwickshire LEA
Jim Grundy, Becta
Linda Evans, David Fulton Publishers

Contributors to the Series

The authors

Mike North is an Information and Communication Technology consultant and has worked with the RNID, NIACE and Becta. He has a background in teaching as an ICT co-ordinator and worked as a teacher of the deaf for eighteen years. He now gives advice and develops training materials to promote the effective use of ICT in all areas of education. He specialises in the use of ICT in deaf education and Adult and Community Learning.

In 2004 he was co-author of an RNID guidelines publication, *Using ICT with Deaf Pupils*, and is a regular contributor to the *British Association for Teachers of the Deaf* magazine.

Sally McKeown works in the inclusion team at Becta and is a consultant for a number of other organisations, including NIACE, Network Training and LSDA. She is also a freelance journalist. Her specialisms include ICT for students with dyslexia, MFL and SEN, and the use of ICT for administration. She writes about learning difficulties for the *Times Educational Supplement* and the *Guardian* and is a columnist for *Special Children* magazine.

In 2001 her book *Unlocking Potential* was shortlisted for the NASEN Special Needs Book Award. Other books include *Computing for the Terrified* (BBC, 1995), *Supporting Children with Dyslexia: Practical Approaches for Teachers and Parents* with Garry Squires (Questions Publishing Co. Ltd 2003), and *Meeting Special Needs in the Modern Foreign Languages Classroom* (David Fulton, 2004).

Series editor

Alan Combes started teaching in South Yorkshire in 1967 and was Head of English at several secondary schools before taking on the role of Head of PSHE as part of being senior teacher at Pindar School, Scarborough. He took early retirement to focus on his writing career and has authored two citizenship textbooks as well as writing several features for the *TES*. He has been used as an adviser on citizenship by the DfES and has emphasised citizenship's importance for special needs pupils as a speaker for NASEN.

SEN specialists

Sue Briggs is a freelance education consultant based in Hereford. She writes and speaks on inclusion, special educational needs and disability, and Autistic Spectrum Disorders, and is a lay member of the SEN and Disability Tribunal. Until recently, she was SEN Inclusion Co-ordinator for Herefordshire Education Directorate. Originally trained as a secondary music teacher, Sue has extensive experience in mainstream and special schools. For six years she was a teacher in charge of a language disorder unit.

Sue Cunningham is a learning support co-ordinator at a large mainstream secondary school in the West Midlands, where she manages a large team of Learning Support teachers and assistants. She has experience of working in both mainstream and special schools and has set up and managed a resource base for pupils with moderate learning difficulties in the mainstream as part of an initiative to promote a more inclusive education for pupils with SEN.

Subject specialists

English

Tim Hurst has been a special educational needs co-ordinator in five schools and is particularly interested in the role and use of language in teaching.

Science

Carol Holden works as a science teacher and assistant SENCO in a mainstream secondary school. She has developed courses for pupils with SEN within science and has gained a graduate diploma and MA in Educational Studies, focusing on SEN.

History

Richard Harris has been teaching since 1989. He has taught in three comprehensive schools, as history teacher, Head of Department and Head of Faculty. He has also worked as teacher consultant for secondary history in West Berkshire.

Ian Luff is assistant headteacher of Kesgrave High School, Suffolk and has been Head of History in three comprehensive schools.

Maths

Brian Sharp is a Key Stage 3 mathematics consultant for Herefordshire. Brian has long experience of working both in special and mainstream schools as a teacher of mathematics. He has a range of management experience, including SENCO, mathematics and ICT co-ordinator.

Design and technology

Louise T. Davies is Principal Officer for Design and Technology at the Qualifications and Curriculum Authority and also a freelance consultant. She is an experienced presenter and author of award-winning resources and books for schools. She chairs the Special Needs Advisory Group for the Design and Technology Association.

Religious education

Dilwyn Hunt has worked as a specialist RE adviser, first in Birmingham and at present in Dudley. He has a wide range of experience in the teaching of RE, including mainstream and special RE.

Music

Victoria Jaquiss is SEN specialist for music with children with emotional and behavioural difficulties in Leeds. She devised a system of musical notation primarily for use with steel pans, for which, in 2002, she was awarded the fellowship of the Royal Society of Arts.

Diane Paterson works as an inclusive music curriculum teacher in Leeds.

Geography

Diane Swift is a project leader for the Geographical Association. Her interest in special needs developed whilst she was a Staffordshire geography adviser and inspector.

PE and sport

Crispin Andrews is an education/sports writer with nine years' experience of teaching and sports coaching.

Art

Kim Earle is Able Pupils Consultant for St Helens and has been a Head of Art and Design. Kim is also a practising designer jeweller.

Gill Curry is Gifted and Talented Strand Co-ordinator for the Wirral. She has twenty years' experience as Head of Art and has also been an art advisory teacher. She is also a practising artist specialising in print.

Modern Foreign Languages

Sally McKeown has responsibility for language-based work in the Inclusion team at Becta. She wrote the MFL Special Needs Materials for CILT's NOF training and writes regularly for the TES, Guardian and Special Children magazines.

Citizenship

Alan Combes has previously authored two citizenship text books as well as writing several features for the TES. He has been used as an adviser on citizenship by the DfES and has emphasised citizenship's importance for special needs pupils as a speaker for NASEN.

Contents of the CD

The CD contains resources which can be amended for individual needs and printed out for use by the purchasing individual or institution. Increasing the font size and spacing will improve accessibility for some students, as will changes in the background colour. Alternatively, print onto pastel-coloured paper for greater ease of reading. Please note that the PowerPoint® presentations were created in Microsoft® Office XP: minor layout changes may occur when other versions of Microsoft Office are used. In order for all features to be enabled, the PowerPoint presentations must be run in Slide Show view.

Staff development and team discussion
INSET Activity 1 (Appendix 1): SEN and Disability Act 2001
INSET Activity 2 (Appendix 2.1): What do we really think?
INSET Activity 3 (Appendix 3.1): Keeping strategies in mind

Sample ICT policy (Appendix 2.2)

Working with Teaching Assistants (Appendix 7)

Classroom resources
Making tea and coffee instructions (two branch)
Two branch template
Flowers and leaves (two choice)
Template for two choice
Template for three choice
Using a CD-ROM with a computer
Costing model for Macbeth

Inclusive environments
Acceptable use policy (Appendix 8)
PowerPoint, the good, the bad and the unintelligible
Organising the layout of an ICT room

Introduction

All children have the right to a good education and the opportunity to fulfil their potential. All teachers should expect to teach children with special educational needs (SEN) and all schools should play their part in educating children from the local community, whatever their background or ability. (*Removing Barriers to Achievement: The Government's Strategy for SEN*, Feb. 2004[1])

It is often argued that computers have made the world smaller and brought communities together. Now we can access information from all around the globe. We can talk online, or via video conferencing, to people we would never have the chance to meet in real life. Information and Communications Technology (ICT) can bring the outside world into the classroom and make the classroom walls dissolve as we all enter the global village. That's the theory and, even when practice does not quite match the rhetoric, it is still exciting to see how the tools can help a child with poor motor skills produce a legible piece of work or find a photograph or piece of clip art to illustrate a concept or bring a project to life. How did we manage before we had this vast treasure trove, just a tantalising few clicks away?

ICT has become the new basic skill. It is not just a subject in its own right at the various key stages, it is also embedded in the curriculum for all subjects. This is exciting but may prove onerous for ICT co-ordinators. Not only are they responsible for the pupils' development and the needs of support staff, but they must also take on board the needs of their colleagues in other subject areas too. A good ICT co-ordinator should be messianic, practical, endlessly patient and have lots of imaginative ideas.

All staff need to be aware of the different ways in which children learn and how to overcome some of the obstacles which stop learning from taking place. Sometimes staff see the problem as lying solely with the child and his or her physical, sensory or cognitive impairments. We are now discovering that often these can be overcome so long as staff are prepared to adapt their teaching style and, their materials, and consider different ways of working. Inaccessible teaching materials or ill-advised grouping of pupils will create stumbling blocks for all pupils, not just those with statements.

In the past, staff relied on the Special Educational Needs Co-ordinator (SENCO) and Teaching Assistants (TAs) to adapt materials and make ideas and activities more manageable for pupils with special needs. In other words, the teacher carried on as usual and someone else acted as intermediary. Now inclusion is everyone's responsibility. The major statutory requirements and non-statutory guidance are summarised in Chapter 1. This sets the context for this resource and provides useful starting points for departmental INSET:

All teaching and non-teaching staff should be involved in the development of the school's SEN policy and be fully aware of the school's procedure for identifying, assessing and making provision for pupils with SEN. ('Table of Roles and Responsibilities', *Code of Practice*, 2002)

Chapter 2 looks at departmental policy for SEN provision and provides useful audit material for reviewing and developing current practice. The term 'special educational needs' or SEN is now widely used and is often vague and meaningless. Does it signify pupils who make slow progress? Truants? Pupils with disabilities but no learning difficulties? All of them? What constitutes special needs in your school?

It is also worth bearing in mind that the descriptions in the staffroom may not be the same as the language of legislation and tribunals! Staff do on occasions – and doubtless under great provocation – describe pupils as 'thick as two short planks', a 'mental case' or 'having the attention span of a goldfish'. Some teachers have subverted the language of special needs so that a child who has problems reading and writing becomes 'dyslexic'; 'ADHD' (Attention Deficit Hyperactivity Disorder) has become a synonym for badly behaved, and a child who seems to be withdrawn or just eccentric is increasingly described as 'autistic'. A little knowledge is indeed a dangerous thing.

There is no doubt that the number of children with special needs being educated in mainstream schools is growing:

> . . . because of the increased emphasis on the inclusion of children with SEN in mainstream schools the number of these children is increasing, as are the severity and variety of their SEN. Children with a far wider range of learning difficulties and variety of medical conditions, as well as sensory difficulties and physical disabilities, are now attending mainstream classes. The implication of this is that mainstream school teachers need to expand their knowledge and skills with regard to the needs of children with SEN. (Stakes and Hornby, 2000[2])

The Code of Practice identifies four main areas of difficulty and these are detailed in Chapter 3 – along with an 'at a glance' guide to a wide range of syndromes and conditions, and guidance on how they might present barriers to learning. The continuing move to greater inclusion means that all teachers can now expect to teach pupils with varied, and quite significant special educational needs at some time. Even five years ago, it was rare to come across children with Asperger's, Down's or Tourette's Syndrome, Autistic Spectrum Disorder, or significant physical/sensory disabilities in community secondary schools. Now, they are entering mainstream education in growing numbers and there is a realisation that their 'inclusion' cannot be simply the responsibility of the SENCO and support staff.

Chapter 4 considers the components of an inclusive classroom and how the layout of the computer room, the structure of the lesson and different ways of presenting teaching materials can make a real difference to pupils with special needs. This theme is extended in Chapter 5 to look more closely at teaching and learning styles and consider ways in which to help all pupils maximise their potential.

Chapter 6 covers different types of assessment. Monitoring pupils' achievements is a key factor in meeting their learning needs. Those pupils who make slower progress than their peers are often working just as hard, or even harder, but their efforts can go unrewarded. Chapter 6 looks at assessment and review and the vexed question of coursework.

Teachers of ICT need help. They need to be able to rely on the technology, and need support with both the pupils and the equipment. Technology support can make the difference between a successful lesson and a disaster. Similarly, Teaching or Learning Support Assistants (TAs, LSAs) can be one of the best resources in the classroom. Chapter 7 looks at how teachers can manage in-class support and build up skills and confidence.

The ICT staff often have a cross-school role too. They will undoubtedly liaise with the SENCO, but may be expected to know about specialist peripherals for pupils with physical disabilities, and be able to recommend software, for example, to support a pupil with a visual impairment in history. Chapter 8 covers some of these issues, and there are useful guides on accessibility as well as a number of case studies in the appendices.

The revised regulations for SEN provision make it clear that mainstream schools are expected to provide for pupils with a wide diversity of needs, and teaching is evaluated on the extent to which all pupils are engaged and enabled to achieve.

This book has been produced in response to the implications of all of this for secondary subject teachers. The authors have considerable experience of the problems facing ICT teachers in schools and a wide knowledge of the power of technology to support pupils with varying needs. The book and accompanying CD provide a resource that can be used with colleagues:

- to shape departmental policy and practice for special needs provision;

- to enable staff to react with a measured response when inclusion issues arise.

This book will not necessarily teach you about ICT. However, it will help you to find ways to involve, encourage and motivate pupils and to extend the ICT learning opportunities for all children in your classes.

References

[1] DfES (2004) *Removing Barriers to Achievement: The Government's Strategy for SEN*. London: DfES.
[2] Stakes, R. and Hornby, G. (2000) *Meeting Special Needs in Mainstream Schools: A Practical Guide for Teachers*. London: David Fulton Publishers.

CHAPTER 1

Meeting Special Educational Needs – Your Responsibility

Inclusion in education involves the process of increasing the participation of students in, and reducing their exclusion from, the cultures, curricula and communities of local schools . . . (Booth and Ainscow, 2000)[1]

Inclusion signifies different things to different people. For some it simply means the presence of a child with disabilities or learning difficulties in a mainstream classroom, alongside other children. But is that inclusion, integration or a pointless exercise in political correctness?

> Nadia has learning difficulties. The class are learning how to make eye-catching posters. She sits next to Duane and watches while he changes the fonts and puts in borders. She asks him questions and keeps up a non-stop stream of chatter.
>
> Frederica also has learning difficulties. She is keen to make a poster for a Jumble Sale at her church. Her Learning Assistant types in the text. Frederica has a handout with six pictures which show her how to edit the font and put a border round the text. She changes the font, font size and colour but gives up on the border.
>
> At the end of the lesson, Frederica has learnt how to change the appearance of text; Nadia has learnt that Duane doesn't like her talking when he is trying to work.

The *Index for Inclusion* was distributed to all maintained schools by the Department for Education and Skills and has been a valuable tool for many schools as they have worked to develop their inclusive practice. It supports schools in the review of their policies, practices and procedures, and the development of an inclusive approach, and where it has been used as part of the school improvement process – looking at inclusion in the widest sense – it has been a great success. For many people however, *The Index* lacked any real teeth, and recent legislation and non-statutory guidance is more authoritative.

The SEN and Disability Act 2001

Billed by the Disability Rights Commission as 'the biggest shake-up of the law in 20 years', the Special Educational Needs and Disability Act (SENDA) gave disabled pupils the right to an education free from discrimination. Now all schools must provide equality of opportunity for children with disabilities and non-disabled pupils.

The Disability Rights Commission states that:

> Since September 2002 schools must ensure that disabled pupils are not treated 'less favourably' and not disadvantaged in every aspect of the life of the school: from teaching and learning to after school clubs; from school organisation to what happens in the dinner queue; from timetabling to the use of classroom support; from homework to anti-bullying policies; from admissions to exclusions.[2]

The Act amended the Disability Discrimination Act and created important new duties for schools:

- to take reasonable steps to ensure that disabled pupils are not placed at a substantial disadvantage in relation to the education and other services they provide. This means they must anticipate where barriers to learning lie and take action to remove them as far as they are able;

- to plan strategically to increase the extent to which disabled pupils can participate in the curriculum, make the physical environment more accessible and ensure that written material is provided in accessible formats.

The reasonable steps taken might include:

- changing policies and practices

- changing course requirements

- changing physical features of a building

- providing interpreters or other support workers

- delivering courses in alternative ways

- providing materials in other formats

- accepting alternative ways of recording

(See Appendix 1 for an activity to support your thinking and staff development.)

Implications for ICT provision

Schools have a planning duty to increase the extent to which pupils with disabilities can participate in the school's curriculum and, in many cases, ICT will offer a range of tools to support access, whether through access devices or through software. Where pupils of any age who have disabilities are expected to use the same machines as other pupils, then there must be a reasonable provision of machines with access technology such as switches, keyboard alternatives, key guards, tracker balls or joysticks. All pupils with impaired vision or literacy problems may reasonably expect to find that they have some access to enlarged text or a speech facility so that they can hear the text that other pupils read. Learners with dyslexia may have personal preferences for fonts, screen colour combinations, styles in Word and web browser options, and should have the facility to save them rather than set them up every time they use a computer.

Depending on the nature and extent of a pupil's disability or learning difficulty, a school may need to provide an initial assessment and develop an individual solution for the student. This legislation relates not just to the classroom but also to other facilities such as the library, gym or careers office, so staff may have to provide adaptations to ensure that the pupil can access any ICT provided anywhere in the school.

The Revised National Curriculum

The Revised National Curriculum (2002) emphasises the provision of effective learning opportunities for all learners, and establishes three principles for promoting inclusion:

- the setting of suitable learning challenges

- responding to pupils' diverse learning needs

- overcoming potential barriers to learning and assessment

The National Curriculum Inclusion Statement suggests that staff may need to differentiate tasks and materials, and facilitate access to learning by:

- encouraging pupils to use all available senses and experiences

- planning for participation in all activities

- helping children to manage their behaviour, take part in learning and prepare for work

- helping pupils to manage their emotions

- giving teachers where necessary, the discretion to teach pupils material from earlier key stages, providing consideration is given to age-appropriate learning contexts

The Qualifications and Curriculum Authority (QCA) has also introduced performance descriptions (P levels/P scales) to enable teachers to observe and record small steps of progress made by some pupils with SEN. These descriptions outline early learning and attainment for each subject in the National Curriculum, including citizenship, RE and PSHE. They chart progress up to NC level 1 through eight steps. The performance descriptions for P1 to P3 are common across all subjects, and are designed for pupils with profound and multiple learning difficulties who need to access the curriculum through sensory activities and experiences. There are two differentiated descriptions within each of levels P1 to P3, termed (i) and (ii) within each level. From level P4, the P scales describe performance related to subject-focused skills, knowledge and understanding. (You can read more about P levels in Chapter 6.)

The Code of Practice for Special Educational Needs

The Revised Code of Practice (implemented in 2002) describes a cyclical process of planning, target setting and review for pupils with special educational needs. It also makes clear the expectation that the vast majority of pupils with special needs will be educated in mainstream settings. Those identified as needing over and above what the school can provide from its own resources, however, are nominated for 'School Action Plus', and outside agencies will be involved in planned intervention. This may involve professionals from the Learning Support Service, a specialist teacher or therapist, or an educational psychologist, working with the school's SENCO to put together an Individual Education Plan (IEP) for the pupil. In a minority of cases (the numbers vary widely between LEAs) pupils may be assessed by a multi-disciplinary team on behalf of the local education authority, whose representatives then decide whether or not to issue a statement of SEN. This is a legally binding document detailing the child's needs and setting out the resources which *must* be provided. It is reviewed every year.

Fundamental principles of the Special Needs code of practice

- A child with special educational needs should have their needs met.

- The special educational needs of children will normally be met in mainstream schools or settings.

- The views of the child should be sought and taken into account.

- Parents have a vital role to play in supporting their child's education.

- Children with special educational needs should be offered full access to a broad, balanced and relevant education, including an appropriate curriculum for the Foundation stage and the National Curriculum.

Ofsted

Ofsted inspectors are required to make judgments about a school's inclusion policy, and how this is translated into practice in individual classrooms.

According to Ofsted (2003) the following key factors help schools to become more inclusive:

- a climate of acceptance of all pupils

- careful preparation of placements for SEN pupils

- availability of sufficient suitable teaching and personal support

- widespread awareness among staff of the particular needs of pupils with SEN and an understanding of the practical ways of meeting these needs in the classroom

- sensitive allocation to teaching groups and careful curriculum modification, timetables and social arrangements

- availability of appropriate materials and teaching aids and adapted accommodation

- an active approach to personal and social development (PSD), as well as to learning

- well-defined and consistently applied approaches to managing difficult behaviour

- assessment, recording and reporting procedures which can embrace and express adequately the progress of pupils with more complex SEN who make only small gains in learning and PSHE

- involving parents/carers as fully as possible in decision-making, keeping them well informed about their child's progress and giving them as much practical support as possible

- developing and taking advantage of training opportunities, including links with special schools and other schools

Special Educational Needs and Disability: Towards Inclusive Schools

The document reports that the Government's revised inclusion framework has contributed to a growing awareness of the benefits of inclusion, and response to it has led to some improvement in practice. Its findings are as follows:

- Most mainstream schools are now committed to meeting special needs.

- A few schools are able to accommodate pupils with complex needs.

- There has been little effect on the proportion of pupils with SEN in mainstream schools.

- There has been little effect on the range of needs for which mainstream schools cater.

- The number of pupils placed in pupil referral units and independent special schools has increased.

The report shows that taking all the steps needed to enable pupils with SEN to participate fully in the life of the school and achieve their potential remains a significant challenge for many schools. Expectations of achievement are often neither well enough defined, nor pitched high enough. Progress in learning remains slower than it should be for a significant number of pupils. Few schools evaluate their provision for pupils with SEN systematically so that they can establish how effective the provision is and whether it represents value for money. At the same time, not enough use is made by mainstream schools of the potential for adapting the curriculum and teaching methods so that pupils have suitable opportunities to improve key skills.

The report also says that the teaching of pupils with SEN is of varying quality, with a high proportion of lessons having shortcomings. Support by Teaching Assistants can be vital, but the organisation of it can mean that pupils have insufficient opportunity to develop their skills, understanding and independence. Despite the helpful contributions by the national strategies, the quality of work to improve the literacy of pupils with SEN remains inconsistent. Effective partnership work between mainstream schools and special schools on curriculum and teaching is the exception rather than the rule. Over half the schools visited had no disability access plans and, of those plans that did exist, the majority focused only on accommodation.

Ofsted concludes that some pupils with SEN continue to face barriers to participation and achievement, including inaccessible premises and shortfalls in support to reach their potential. They are more likely to be persistent non-attenders and to be permanently excluded than other pupils. Many of those in mainstream schools could do better, if the curriculum, teaching and other support were better adapted to their needs, and greater rigour was applied to setting and pursuing targets for achievement. Until more is expected from the lowest-attaining pupils, improvement in provision for pupils with SEN and in the standards they reach will continue to be slow.[3]

Table 1.1 on page 12 provides a summary of recent SEN legislation and DfES guidance.

Removing Barriers

Effective teaching for pupils with special educational needs is, by and large, effective for all pupils, but as schools become more inclusive, teachers need to be able to respond to a wider range of needs. The Government's strategy for SEN (*Removing Barriers to Learning*, 2004) sets out ambitious proposals to 'help teachers expand their repertoire of inclusive skills and strategies and plan confidently to include children with increasingly complex needs'.

In many cases, pupils' individual needs will be met through greater differentiation of tasks and materials, i.e. school-based intervention as set out in the SEN Code of Practice. A smaller number of pupils may need access to specialist equipment and approaches or to alternative or adapted activities, as part of a School Action Plus programme, augmented by advice and support from external specialists. The QCA, on its website (2003), encourages teachers to take specific action to provide access to learning for pupils with special educational needs by:

(a) providing for pupils who need help with communication, language and literacy, through:

- using texts that pupils can read and understand
- using visual and written materials in different formats, including large print, symbol text and Braille
- using ICT, other technological aids and taped materials
- using alternative and augmentative communication, including signs and symbols
- using translators, communicators and amanuenses

(b) planning, where necessary, to develop pupils' understanding through the use of all available senses and experiences by:

- using materials and resources that pupils can access through sight, touch, sound, taste or smell
- using word descriptions and other stimuli to make up for a lack of first-hand experiences
- using ICT, visual and other materials to increase pupils' knowledge of the wider world
- encouraging pupils to take part in everyday activities such as play, drama, class visits and exploring the environment

(c) planning for pupils' full participation in learning and in physical and practical activities by:

- using specialist aids and equipment
- providing support from adults or peers when needed
- adapting tasks or environments
- providing alternative activities, where necessary

(d) helping pupils to manage their behaviour, to take part in learning effectively and safely, and, at Key Stage 4, to prepare for work by:

- setting realistic demands and stating them explicitly
- using positive behaviour management, including a clear structure of rewards and sanctions
- giving pupils every chance and encouragement to develop the skills they need to work well with a partner or a group
- teaching pupils to value and respect the contribution of others
- encouraging and teaching independent working skills
- teaching essential safety rules

TABLE 1.1 LEGISLATION AND DFES GUIDANCE

Title	What it says about Inclusion	What Teachers Need to do	Assessment and Management Issues
SENDA	• Disabled pupils have the right to an education free from discrimination.	• Take reasonable steps to ensure that disabled pupils are not placed at a substantial disadvantage in relation to the education and other services they provide. • Anticipate where barriers to learning lie and take action to remove them.	• Plan strategically to increase the extent to which disabled pupils can participate in the curriculum, make the physical environment more accessible and ensure that written material is provided in accessible formats.
The Revised National Curriculum (2002)	Establishes three principles for promoting inclusion: • setting suitable learning challenges • responding to pupils' diverse learning needs • overcoming potential barriers to learning and assessment.	Differentiate tasks and materials, and facilitate access to learning by: • encouraging pupils to use all available senses and experiences • planning for participation in all activities • helping children to manage their behaviour, take part in learning and prepare for work • helping pupils to manage their emotions • giving teachers, where necessary, the discretion to teach pupils material from earlier key stages, providing consideration is given to age-appropriate learning contexts.	• QCA have performance descriptions (P levels/P scales) to record small steps of progress made by some pupils with SEN up to NC level 1 through eight steps. P1 to P3 outline the types and range of general performance that some pupils with learning difficulties may demonstrate. From level P4 onwards, performance is described in terms of subject-focused skills, knowledge and understanding.
The Code of Practice for Special Educational Needs	• A child with special educational needs should have their needs met. • The special educational needs of children will normally be met in mainstream schools or settings. • The views of the child should be sought and taken into account.	• Ensure that there is a cyclical process of planning, target setting and review for pupils with special educational needs.	• There should be an expectation that the vast majority of pupils with special needs will be educated in mainstream settings. • 'School Action Plus' outside agencies should work with the SENCO to put together an IEP for the pupil.

- Parents have a vital role to play in supporting their child's education.
- Children with special educational needs should be offered full access to a broad, balanced and relevant education, including an appropriate curriculum for the Foundation stage and the National Curriculum.
- A minority of pupils may be assessed by a multi-disciplinary team on behalf of the local education authority whose representatives then decide whether or not to issue a statement of SEN. This is a legally binding document detailing the child's needs and setting out the resources which should be provided. It is reviewed every year.

Ofsted (2003)

Inclusion involves:

- a climate of acceptance of all pupils
- availability of appropriate materials and teaching aids and adapted accommodation
- an active approach to personal and social development, as well as to learning
- widespread awareness among staff of the particular needs of SEN pupils and an understanding of the practical ways of meeting these needs in the classroom.
- Ensure sensitive allocation to teaching groups and careful curriculum modification, timetables and social arrangements.
- Involve parents/carers as fully as possible in decision-making, keeping them well informed about their child's progress and giving them as much practical support as possible.
- Develop and take advantage of training opportunities, including links with special schools and other schools. (See Appendix 1 for key points from inspections.)
- Ensure that there are well-defined and consistently applied approaches to managing difficult behaviour.
- Assessment, recording and reporting procedures should embrace and express adequately the progress of pupils with more complex SEN who make only small gains in learning and PSD.
- There should be careful preparation of placements for SEN pupils.
- Sufficient suitable teaching and personal support should be available.

Ofsted's Special educational needs and disability: Towards inclusive schools (Oct 2004)

- There has been little effect on the proportion of pupils with SEN in mainstream schools.
- There has been little effect on the range of needs for which mainstream schools cater.
- The number of pupils placed in pupil referral units and independent special schools has increased.
- Adapt the curriculum and teaching methods so that pupils have suitable opportunities to improve key skills.
- Adapt the curriculum, teaching and other support to meet needs.
- Ensure more rigorous setting of and pursuing of targets for achievement.
- Have higher expectations of achievement.
- Progress remains slower than it should be for a significant number of pupils.
- Evaluate their provision for pupils with SEN more systematically.
- Establish how effective the provision is and whether it represents value for money.
- Put in place disability access plans which do not just focus on accommodation.

(e) helping individuals to manage their emotions, particularly trauma or stress, and to take part in learning by:

- identifying aspects of learning in which the pupil will engage and plan short-term, easily achievable goals in selected activities
- providing positive feedback to reinforce and encourage learning and build self-esteem
- selecting tasks and materials sensitively to avoid unnecessary stress for the pupil
- creating a supportive learning environment in which the pupil feels safe and is able to engage with learning
- allowing time for the pupil to engage with learning and gradually increasing the range of activities and demands

Teacher interventions

Not all pupils with disabilities will necessarily have special educational needs. Many learn alongside their peers with little need for additional resources beyond the aids which they use as part of their daily life, such as a wheelchair, a hearing aid or equipment to aid vision. Teachers must ensure, however, that these pupils can participate as fully and effectively as possible in the curriculum. Teachers should:

- take account of the very slow pace at which some pupils will be able to record work, either manually or with specialist equipment, and of the physical effort required

- be aware of the high levels of concentration necessary for some pupils when following or interpreting text or graphics, particularly when using vision aids or tactile methods, and of the tiredness which may result

- allocate sufficient time, opportunity and access to equipment for pupils to gain information. Alternatively, develop an overlay with key website addresses for pupils to click on. This will save them the trouble of typing in addresses and means they can focus on the content of a website

- be aware of the effort required by some pupils to follow oral work, whether through use of residual hearing, lip reading or a signer, and of the tiredness or loss of concentration which may occur. Make sure there are simple worksheets with visual instructions as an alternative to oral instructions to support deaf learners. This will also benefit those with limited concentration or learning difficulties

- provide notes/worksheets in an electronic form for support staff to refer to before the lesson and pupils to refer to after the lesson

- organise portable storage so pupils/support staff can have access to information away from school, e.g. USB pen storage or CD-ROM

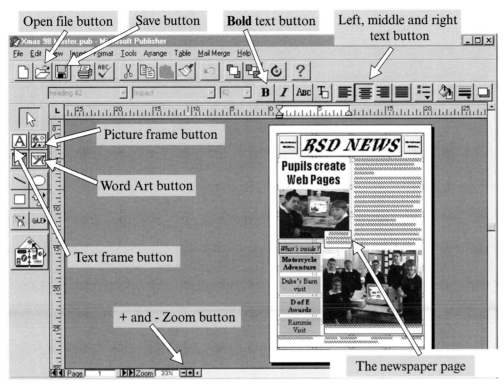

Visual explanation

- plan some opportunities, where necessary, for the development of skills in practical aspects of the curriculum. This might involve providing alternative or adapted activities for control technology for pupils who are unable to manipulate sensors such as onscreen software-based control technology activities

- ensure that all pupils can be included and participate safely in outside visits, for example to collect data

- identify aspects of Programmes of Study and attainment targets that may present specific difficulties for individuals, and identify solutions

- provide assistive writing packages for pupils who have problems composing text, for whatever reason. These might include predictive word-processing packages, whole-word processing facilities, planning tools or writing frames. Others may require a symbol word processor in order to communicate in text form and provide written evidence of their capabilities. *Writing With Symbols* from Widget and *Clicker 4* from Crick Software are particularly recommended

- help visually impaired pupils to learn about fonts and formatting by providing tactile examples so they can feel the difference between bold and italic and have some sense of how and why they might be used in a document.

Ten good things about ICT in the inclusive classroom

1. Many learners like computers and find them motivating.

2. Multimedia means that information can be accessed through text, graphics or sound to suit the students' individual learning styles and strengths.

3. Software which combines colour, pictures, animations, sound and humour can grab pupils who are turned off by group work and listening.

4. ICT offers an opportunity for social interaction. Students can work together around the computer, focusing on the learning task. Through this medium they can develop their language and social skills as well as learn from one another.

5. Keyboards of all shapes and sizes and switches offer access to word processing so that work is legible.

6. Predictive packages can make the difference between thoughts in the head and words on the page.

7. Spell checkers may make the difference between chaos and meaning.

8. ICT provides a range of assistive technology tools. Hardware and software help many pupils with physical, sensory and learning difficulties to overcome barriers.

9. Drawing tools mean that staff can easily develop and provide visual instruction sheets for pupils who have problems getting information from listening or reading.

10. Digital cameras allow pupils to record experiences and achievements in a very immediate way.

Being an advocate

Certainly ICT is the one subject where pupils with disabilities should, and often can, operate on a level playing field with other children. Computers are designed to provide universal access in the business world. Let's make it happen in schools too.

References

[1] Booth, T. and Ainscow, M. (2000) *The Index for Inclusion*. Centre for Studies on Inclusive Education, New Redland, Frenchay Campus, Coldharbour Lane, Bristol BS16 1QU. Tel: +44 117344 4007.

[2] Disability Rights Commission. Website: http://www.drc-gb.org/education/news/newsdetails.asp?id=709&section=1

[3] *Special educational needs and disability: Towards inclusive schools*. Available at: http://www.ofsted.gov.uk/publications/index.cfm?fuseaction=pubs.summary&id=3737

CHAPTER 2

Departmental Policy

A good departmental policy describes a strategy for meeting pupils' special educational needs within the particular curricular area. It is not just a document you have ready for when an inspector calls. The process of getting staff together to clarify and evaluate current ideas and practice within the ICT team is far more important than the resultant piece of paper. It gives everyone a chance to reflect on what they are trying to achieve and to establish a consistent approach.

> The starting point will be the school's SEN policy as required by the Education Act 1996, with each subject department 'fleshing out' the detail in a way which describes how things work in practice. The policy should establish:
>
> - the curriculum and how it can be differentiated
>
> - who is responsible for which areas
>
> - arrangements for assessment and reporting
>
> - staff with specialist training and/or knowledge
>
> - guidelines for working effectively with support staff
>
> - staff training needs

Where to start when writing a policy

Many schools find an audit a useful starting point. This involves gathering information and reviewing current practice with regard to pupils with SEN. It should be completed by all teaching staff in the department, preferably with some additional advice from the SENCO or another member of staff with responsibility for SEN within the school. Some schools like to involve support staff, while others prefer to restrict input to teaching staff.

An audit should be seen as an exercise in sharing good practice and encouraging joint planning, not as a punitive measure or another 'good idea'. Before embarking on an audit, it is worth investing some time in a department meeting or training day, to raise awareness of special educational needs and disability legislation and establish a shared philosophy. (Appendix 2.1 contains OHT layouts and an activity to use with staff. These are also on the accompanying CD, with additional exercises you may choose to use. Appendix 2.2 has a departmental policy for you to discuss, criticise and adapt.)

The following headings may be useful in establishing a working policy:

General statement

- What does legislation and DfES guidance say?

- What does the school policy state?

- What do members of the department have to do to comply with it?

Definition of SEN

- What does SEN mean?

- What are the areas of need and the categories used in the Code of Practice?

- Are there any special implications within the subject area?

Provision for staff within the department

- How is information shared?

- Who has responsibility for SEN within the department?

- How and when is information shared?

- Where and what information is stored?

Provision for pupils with SEN

- How are pupils with SEN assessed and monitored in the department?

- How are contributions to IEPs and reviews made?

- What criteria are used for organising teaching groups?

- What alternative courses are offered to pupils with SEN?

- How are barriers to access to the curriculum reduced or eliminated?

- How are the needs of pupils with physical difficulties or sensory impairments met as regards access to the site?

- What special internal and external examination arrangements are made?

- What guidance is available for working with support staff?

The law requires schools to anticipate the needs of disabled pupils and disabled potential pupils and the adjustments they could be making for them. A departmental policy should make staff aware of the requirements of SENDA and the ways they can take reasonable steps to prevent pupils being placed at a 'substantial disadvantage'. The accessibility options on a computer can be tailored to meet the specific needs of a user. This facility may benefit many SEN pupils and, indeed, may be essential for them to access the computer and operate it effectively.

> Janine has some problems with visual tracking. She finds it easier to work with a yellow background on all text documents and requires the text size for web pages to be set to 'large'.
>
> Naresh needs the mouse pointer to be set to the slowest setting and the numeric keypad to be enabled for pointer control.

This is fine when these pupils are in the special needs department as the teacher or TA can adjust the accessibility profiles on their stand-alone computer. However, when Janine and Naresh use the school network, it is not possible to change the accessibility options as neither staff nor pupils have 'permission' to alter network settings. This is a common situation and it is quite understandable that network security is configured to ensure things are not 'fiddled with', but there should be a procedure in place to allow individual accessibility profiles to be set up.

The ICT department is in an ideal position to develop a system that allows pupils to have user profiles tailored to their specific needs. This is particularly important where pupils move around a school and log on to the network in a variety of locations. Initially this may mean more work for the network manager but, once established, roving profiles can be given to all those with special needs, and they will be able to log on to the network in any location and get the options they require. In the long term this will save a lot of staff time and frustration and help build the confidence and self-image of the pupil.

Resources and learning materials

- Is there any specialist equipment used in the department?

- How are resources developed?

- Where are resources stored?

Qualifications and Continuing Professional Development needs

- What qualifications do the members of the department have?

- What training has taken place?

- How is training planned?

- Is a record kept of training completed and training needs?

An ICT teacher discusses the possibility of setting up access profiles with Grant, the ICT technician.

Sue: I've got three pupils in my ICT classes who would really find life easier if we could change things like the mouse speed, background colours and text size to suit their needs.

Grant: It's fairly easy on a stand-alone computer to create a local profile but a bit trickier if you want to change any of the network machines.

Sue: I think they need a consistent set-up that gives them the same options each time they log on, no matter where they are in the school. Jenny needs a trailing pointer, Harry prefers a yellow background to his text documents and Bhavini needs access to her text-reading software. What do they do in other schools?

Grant: Every school network set-up is different. When a pupil logs on to a computer they are only allowed access to their own files and a certain set of programs. Pupils and staff are not usually allowed to access the area where settings can be changed. It is possible to set up a profile specifically for a user with all the settings they require.

Sue: That's what we need. How long will it take?

Grant: It depends what is needed for each profile. I would think about half an hour of fiddling to set up each mandatory profile on the server. Or we could set up roaming profiles for all those who need special settings.

Sue: What's the difference, and which would work best?

Grant: Well, a mandatory profile would need setting up for each individual user, with settings appropriate for their needs. These would be fixed, and the user would not be able to alter them again after creation. Another option with a mandatory profile would be to give the user access to settings, e.g. mouse pointers and backgrounds, so they can set them as desired for that logon. These settings, however, would not be saved at logoff and would require setting again next time the user logs on.

A roaming profile will give the user the ability to tailor their environment whilst logged on. The settings will be saved to the network at logoff making the profile accessible from any network PC. Logon times with a roaming profile can be slightly longer but this can be outweighed by the benefits to the user and the shorter initial creation time for technical support staff.[1]

---

[1] *Technical support and information for ICT technicians can be found at:*
http://support.microsoft.com/?kbid=243420
http://support.microsoft.com/?kbid=323368
http://www.microsoft.com/technet/prodtechnol/windows2000serv/deploy/confeat/09w2kadb.mspx

Monitoring and reviewing the policy

- How will the policy be monitored?

- When will the policy be reviewed?

The content of a SEN departmental policy

This section gives detailed information on what a SEN policy might include. Each heading is expanded with some detailed information and raises the main issues with regard to teaching pupils with SEN. At the end of each section there is an example statement. The example statements can be personalised and brought together to make a policy. All the examples in this chapter are gathered as an example policy in Appendix 2.3.

General statement with reference to the school's SEN policy

All schools must have a SEN policy according to the Education Act 1996. This policy will set out basic information on the school's SEN provision, and how the school identifies, assesses and provides for pupils with SEN, including information on staffing, and working in partnership with other professionals and parents.

Any department policy needs to have reference to the school SEN policy.

Example

> All members of the department will ensure that the needs of all pupils with SEN are met, according to the aims of the school and its SEN policy.

Provision for staff within the department

In many schools, each department nominates a member of staff to have special responsibility for SEN provision (with or without remuneration). This can be very effective where there is a system of regular liaison between department SEN representatives and the SENCO in the form of meetings or paper communications or a mixture of both.

The responsibilities of this post may include liaison between the department and the SENCO, attending any liaison meetings and providing feedback via meetings and minutes, attending training, maintaining the departmental SEN information and records and representing the need of pupils with SEN at departmental level. This post can be seen as a valuable development opportunity for staff. The name of this person should be included in the policy.

Setting out how members of the department raise concerns about pupils with SEN can be included in this section. Concerns may be raised at specified departmental meetings before referral to the SENCO. An identified member of the department could make referrals to the SENCO and keep a record of this information.

Reference to working with support staff will include a commitment to planning and communication between staff. There may be information on inviting support staff to meetings, resources and lesson plans.

A reference to the centrally held lists of pupils with SEN and other relevant information will also be included in this section. A note about confidentiality of information should be included.

Example

The member of staff with responsibility for overseeing the provision of SEN within the department will attend liaison meetings and feed back to other members of the department. He/she will maintain the department's SEN information file, attend appropriate training and disseminate this to all departmental staff. All information will be treated with confidentiality.

Provision for pupils with SEN

It is the responsibility of all staff to know which pupils have SEN and to identify any pupils having difficulties. Pupils with SEN may be identified by staff within the department in a variety of ways. These may be listed and could include:

- observation in lessons
- assessment of class work
- homework tasks
- end of module tests
- progress checks
- annual examinations
- reports

Setting out how pupils with SEN are grouped within the ICT department may include specifying the criteria used and/or the philosophy behind the method of grouping.

Example

> The pupils are grouped according to ability as informed by Key Stage 2 results, reading scores and any other relevant performance, or social information.
>
> Monitoring arrangements and details of how pupils can move between groups should also be set out. Information collected may include:
>
> ● National Curriculum levels
>
> ● departmental assessments
>
> ● reading scores
>
> ● advice from pastoral staff
>
> ● discussion with staff in the SEN dept
>
> ● information provided on IEPs

Special examination arrangements need to be considered not only at Key Stages 3 and 4 but also for internal examinations. How and when these will be discussed should be clarified. Reference to the SENCO and examination arrangements from the examination board should be taken into account. Ensuring that staff in the department understand the current legislation and guidance from central government is important, so a reference to the SEN Code of Practice and the levels of SEN intervention is helpful within the policy. Here is a good place also to put a statement about the school behaviour policy and rewards and sanctions, and how the department will make any necessary adjustments to meet the needs of pupils with SEN.

Example

> It is understood that pupils with SEN may receive additional support if they have a statement of SEN, are at School Action Plus or School Action. The staff in the ICT department will aim to support the pupils to achieve their targets as specified on their IEPs and will provide feedback for IEP or statement reviews. Pupils with SEN will be included in the departmental monitoring system used for all pupils. Additional support will be requested as appropriate.

Resources and learning materials

The department policy needs to specify what differentiated materials are available, where they are kept and how to find new resources. This section could include a statement about working with support staff to develop resources or access specialist resources as needed, and the use of ICT. Teaching strategies may also be identified if appropriate. Advice on more specialist equipment can be sought as necessary, possibly through LEA support services: contact details may be available from the SENCO, or the department may have direct links. Any specially bought subject text or alternative/appropriate courses can be specified as well as any external assessment and examination courses.

Example

> The department will provide suitably differentiated materials and, where appropriate, specialist resources for pupils with SEN. Additional texts are available for those pupils working below National Curriculum level 3. At Key Stage 4, an alternative course to GCSE is offered at Entry level but, where possible, pupils with SEN will be encouraged to reach their full potential and follow a GCSE course. Support staff will be provided with curriculum information in advance of lessons and will also be involved in lesson planning. A list of resources is available in the department handbook and on the noticeboard.

Health and safety issues

Health and safety issues surrounding the use of ICT are important for all pupils, but there are areas where special consideration must be given to the needs of SEN pupils. Specific recommendations and guidance for staff should be included in the department SEN policy. (See Appendix 2.4 for a sample.)

Qualifications and Continuing Professional Development needs

It is important to recognise and record the qualifications and special skills gained by staff within the department. Training can include not only external courses but also in-house INSET and opportunities such as observing other staff, working to produce materials with other staff, and visiting other establishments. Staff may have hidden skills that might enhance the work of the department and the school, for example some staff might be proficient in the use of sign language.

Example

> A record of training undertaken, specialist skills and training required will be kept in the department handbook. Requests for training will be considered in line with the department and school improvement plan.

Monitoring and reviewing the policy

To be effective any policy needs regular monitoring and review. These can be planned as part of the yearly cycle. The responsibility for the monitoring can rest with the Head of Department but will have more effect if supported by someone from outside acting as a critical friend. This could be the SENCO or a member of the senior management team in school.

Example

> The department SEN policy will be monitored by the Head of Department on a planned annual basis, with advice being sought from the SENCO as part of a three-yearly review process.

Conclusion

Creating a departmental SEN policy should be a developmental activity to improve the teaching and learning for all pupils but especially for those with special or additional needs. The policy should be a working document that will evolve and change; it is there to challenge current practice and to encourage improvement for both pupils and staff. If departmental staff work together to create the policy, they will have ownership of it; it will have true meaning and be effective in clarifying practice.

Different Types of SEN

This chapter is a starting point for information on the special educational needs most frequently occurring in the mainstream secondary school. Labels are, of course, fraught with danger. Teachers bandy about a term such as ADHD or dyslexic as verbal shorthand. The danger is that the label sticks: a child may not have ADHD but be troubled and insecure. Many children have been labelled 'dyslexic' when they are long sighted or have a degree of hearing loss which makes phonics a bit of a mystery.

There is also a danger of spotting all sorts of conditions which seem to apply to pupils you know. This is a variation on hypochondria. The more symptoms you read about, the more you see them everywhere you look! Remember also that a pupil is an individual and not a collection of symptoms and syndromes. Nearly every child is in part atypical of a particular learning difficulty or disability. There are children with hearing loss who have an exceptionally sophisticated grasp of language and syntax, and learners with dyslexia who have clear attractive handwriting.

Nevertheless, this chapter will be a useful starting point for thinking about children you work with. It describes the main characteristics of each learning difficulty and suggests how and why ICT may benefit the pupil. There are also contacts for further information. Try the activity in Appendix 3.1 as a way into thinking about children you work with. As you are reading through the examples, think about how you can change the environment. The child may be a 'square peg in a round hole'. The hole has to change as well as the peg. What can be altered, adapted, made more user-friendly? Don't think, 'Susan has a very limited attention span.' Instead, think about how you will maximise the time she is on task, what back up/support you will give her for when she revisits work, e.g. notes etc., and how you can use ICT to grab her attention and extend the time that she concentrates in your lessons. Appendix 3.2 has case studies of individual children who exhibit some of the characteristics described in this chapter.

Definition of SEN

The special educational needs in this chapter are grouped under the headings used in the SEN Code of Practice (DfES 2001):

- cognition and learning
- behavioural, emotional and social development
- communication and interaction
- sensory and/or physical needs

TABLE 3.1 THE FOUR AREAS OF SEN

Cognition and Learning Needs	Behavioural, Emotional and Social Development Needs	Communication and Interaction Needs	Sensory and/or Physical Needs
Specific learning Difficulties (SpLD)	Behavioural, emotional and social difficulties (BESD)	Speech, language and communication needs	Hearing impairment (HI)
Dyslexia	Attention Deficit Disorder (ADD)	Autistic Spectrum Disorder (ASD)	Visual impairment (VI)
Moderate learning difficulties (MLD)	Attention Deficit Hyperactivity Disorder (ADHD)	Asperger's Syndrome	Multi-sensory impairment (MSI)
Severe learning difficulties (SLD)			Physical difficulties (PD)
Profound and multiple learning difficulties (PMLD)			

COGNITION AND LEARNING NEEDS

Specific Learning Difficulties (SpLD)

The term 'specific learning difficulties' covers dyslexia, dyscalculia and dyspraxia.

Dyslexia

The term 'dyslexia' is used to describe a learning difficulty associated with words and it can affect a pupil's ability to read, write and/or spell. Research has shown that there is no one definitive definition of dyslexia or one identified cause, and it has a wide range of symptoms. Although found across a whole range of ability levels, the idea that dyslexia presents as a difficulty between expected outcomes and performance is widely held.

Main characteristics:

- The pupil may frequently lose their place when reading, make a lot of errors with the high frequency words, have difficulty reading names, and have difficulty blending sounds and segmenting words. Reading requires a great deal of effort and concentration.

- The pupil's work may seem messy with crossing outs, similarly shaped letters may be confused, such as b/d, p/q, m/w, n/u, and letters in words may be jumbled, such as tired/tried. Spelling difficulties often persist into adult life and these pupils become reluctant writers.

How can the subject teacher help?

- Be aware of the type of difficulty and the pupil's strengths.
- Teach and allow the use of word processing, spell checkers and computer-aided learning packages.
- Provide word lists and photocopies of copying from the board.
- Consider alternative recording methods, e.g. pictures, plans, flow charts, mind maps.
- Allow extra time for tasks, including assessments and examinations.

How can ICT help this group of pupils?

- Notes and reminders on a computer can develop their memory skills.
- Planning tools can help learners to organise their thoughts.
- Word processors help to produce legible text.

- Predictive word processors speed up composition.

- Spellcheckers aid correct spelling.

- Talking word processors let the learner hear text.

- Voice recognition may be a useful alternative input.

Dyscalculia

The term 'dyscalculia' is used to describe a difficulty in mathematics. This might be either a marked discrepancy between the pupil's developmental level and general ability on measures of specific maths ability or a total inability to abstract or consider concepts and numbers.

Main characteristics:

- In numeracy, the pupil may have difficulty counting by rote, writing or reading numbers, miss out or reverse numbers, have difficulty with mental maths, and be unable to remember concepts, rules and formulae.

- In maths-based concepts, pupils may have difficulty with money, telling the time, with directions, right and left, or with sequencing events, or may lose track of turns, e.g. in team games, dance.

How can the subject teacher help?

- Provide number/word/rule/formulae lists and photocopies of copying from the board.

- Make use of ICT and teach the use of calculators.

- Encourage the use of rough paper for working out.

- Plan the setting out of work with it well spaced on the page.

- Provide practical objects that are age appropriate to aid learning.

- Allow extra time for tasks, including assessments and examinations.

How can ICT help this group of pupils?

- may improve short-term memory, attention span and sequencing skills.

- can provide auditory feedback.

- can help develop a 'what if' approach instead of always looking for the right answer.

- modelling – pupils see it on screen so develop a sense of the concept.

Dyspraxia

The term 'dyspraxia' is used to describe an immaturity with the way in which the brain processes information, resulting in messages not being properly transmitted.

Main characteristics:

- difficulty in co-ordinating movements, may appear awkward and clumsy

- difficulty with handwriting and drawing, throwing and catching

- difficulty following sequential events, e.g. multiple instructions

- may misinterpret situations, take things literally

- limited social skills resulting in frustration and irritability

- some articulation difficulties

How can the subject teacher help?

- Be sensitive to the pupil's limitations in games and outdoor activities and plan tasks to enable success.

- Ask the pupil questions to check his understanding of instructions/tasks.

- Check seating position to encourage good presentation (both feet resting on the floor, desk at elbow height and with, ideally, a sloping surface to work on).

How can ICT help this group of pupils?

- improves presentation

- can offer privacy

- can accommodate differing learning styles

- gives more control of pupils' own learning

- can motivate pupils to make a greater effort

- may give instant feedback to their responses

The British Dyslexia Association
Tel: 0118 966 8271 Website: www.bda-dyslexia.org.uk
Dyslexia Institute
Tel: 07184 222 300 Website: www.dyslexia-inst.org.uk
Dyspraxic Foundation, 8 West Alley, Hitchin, Herts SG5 1EG
Tel: 01462 454986 (Helpline)
Website: www.dyspraxiafoundation.org.uk
Website: www.dyscalculia.co.uk

Moderate Learning Difficulties (MLD)

The term 'moderate learning difficulties' is used to describe pupils who find it extremely difficult to achieve expected levels of attainment across the curriculum, even with a differentiated and flexible approach. These pupils do not find learning easy and can suffer from low self-esteem and sometimes exhibit unacceptable behaviour as a way of avoiding failure.

Main characteristics:

- difficulties with reading, writing and comprehension
- unable to understand and retain basic mathematical skills and concepts
- immature social and emotional skills
- limited vocabulary and communication skills
- short attention span
- under-developed co-ordination skills
- lack of logical reasoning
- inability to transfer and apply skills to different situations
- difficulty remembering what has been taught
- difficulty with organising themselves, following a timetable, remembering books and equipment
- often lacking in confidence
- may have difficulties with memory

How can the subject teacher help?

- Revisit ideas and concepts regularly as the pupil may be 'a quick forgetter'.
- Check the pupil's strengths, weaknesses and attainment levels.
- Establish a routine within the lesson.
- Keep tasks short and varied.
- Keep listening tasks short or broken up with activities.
- Check previously gained knowledge and build on it.
- Repeat information in different ways.
- Show the child what to do or what the expected outcome is; demonstrate or show examples of completed work.

- Use practical, concrete, visual examples to illustrate explanations.

- Question the pupil to check they have grasped a concept or can follow instructions.

- Make sure the pupil always has something to do.

- Use lots of praise, instant rewards – catch them trying hard.

Matthew Y9 Cognitive and learning difficulties

Often in class Matthew sits and does nothing, just stares into space.
His work is messy and there is no substance to anything he does, which makes it hard for teachers to suggest a way forward, or indeed to find anything to praise.

Skill: Developing ideas and making things happen

Use onscreen Logo software to control a turtle.
   It is important to give Matthew the opportunity to make decisions and develop ideas. The structured approach to using onscreen turtle software will allow him to start with a simple concept like instructing the turtle to move forward and lead to drawing shapes and repeat patterns.
   Matthew will initially need the support of a TA and encouragement to decide how far to move the turtle, when to change direction and what line colour to use.
   The work Matthew creates can be viewed on screen or printed out, the 'professional looking' results will give staff an opportunity for praise.

(You can read more about Matthew in Appendix 3.2.)

How can ICT help this group of pupils?

- word lists, writing frames, shorten text

- provides alternative methods of recording information, e.g. drawings, charts, labelling, diagrams, use of ICT

- multimedia can make things easier to understand

- structured drill and practice software provides reinforcement

- presentation is improved

- easy to revisit work and add an extra bit

The MLD Alliance, c/o The Elfrida Society, 34 Islington Park Street, London N1 1PX
Website: www.mldalliance.com/executive.htm

Down's Syndrome (DS)

Down's Syndrome is the most common identifiable cause of learning disability. This is a genetic condition caused by the presence of an extra chromosome 21. People with DS have varying degrees of learning difficulties, ranging from mild to severe. They have a specific learning profile with characteristic strengths and weaknesses. All share certain physical characteristics but will also inherit family traits, in physical features and personality. They may have additional sight, hearing, respiratory and heart problems.

Main characteristics:

- delayed motor skills
- take longer to learn and consolidate new skills
- limited concentration
- difficulties with generalisation, thinking and reasoning
- sequencing difficulties
- stronger visual than aural skills
- better social than academic skills

How can the subject teacher help?

- Speak directly to the pupil and reinforce with facial expression, pictures and objects.
- Use simple, familiar language in short sentences.
- Check instructions have been understood.
- Give time to process information and formulate a response.
- Break lessons up into a series of shorter, varied, and achievable tasks.
- Accept other ways of recording; drawings, tape/video recordings, symbols, etc.
- Set differentiated tasks linked to the work of the rest of the class.
- Provide age-appropriate resources and activities.
- Provide a 'work buddy'.
- Expect unsupported work for part of each lesson.

How can ICT help this group of pupils?

- Talking word processors mean pupils can read what they have written and not get too hung up on decoding text.

- If learners have difficulties getting information from looking or listening, multimedia can be a good tool. The combination of moving images, graphics, text and sound enable the use of all their senses to reinforce learning.

- Overlay keyboards or on-screen grids enable learners to use symbols or other support alongside traditional text.

- A picture may be worth a 1,000 words and is a lot quicker to process. Lots of clip art and photos on the Web will support understanding.

The Down's Association, 155 Mitcham Road, London SW17 9PG
Tel: 0845 230 0372
Email: info@downs-syndrome.org.uk
Website: http://www.downs-syndrome.org.uk

Fragile X Syndrome

Fragile X Syndrome is caused by a malformation of the X chromosome and is the most common form of inherited learning disability. This intellectual disability varies widely, with up to a third of people affected having learning problems ranging from moderate to severe. More boys than girls are affected but both may be carriers.

Main characteristics:

- delayed and disordered speech and language development

- difficulties with the social use of language

- articulation and/or fluency difficulties

- verbal skills better developed than reasoning skills

- repetitive or obsessive behaviour such as hand-flapping, chewing, etc.

- clumsiness and fine motor co-ordination problems

- attention deficit and hyperactivity

- easily anxious or overwhelmed in busy environments

How can the subject teacher help?

- Liaise with parents.

- Make sure the pupil knows what is to happen in each lesson – provide visual timetables, work schedules or written lists.

- Ensure the pupil sits at the front of the class, in the same seat for all lessons.

- Arrange a work/subject buddy.

- Where possible, keep to routines and give prior warning of all changes.

- Make instructions clear and simple.

- Use visual supports: objects, pictures, symbols.

- Allow the pupil to use a computer to record and access information.

- Give lots of praise and positive feedback.

- Be aware that these pupils are likely to be inattentive, easily distracted, impulsive and overactive. This is not deliberate naughtiness on their part.

How can ICT help this group of pupils?

- Touch screens can help pupils who may prefer to make simple selections on screen, rather than use a keyboard and mouse which are detached from the screen.

- Speech feedback provides information without using text.

- Early switch activities which involve making choices can be a useful way of assessing knowledge.

Fragile X Society, Rood End House, 6 Stortford Road, Dunmow, CM6 1DA
Tel: 01424 813147 (Helpline) Tel: 01371 875100 (Office)
Email: info@fragilex.org.uk Website: http://www.fragilex.org.uk

---

Severe learning difficulties

This term covers a wide and varied group of pupils who have significant intellectual or cognitive impairments. Many have communication difficulties and/or sensory impairments in addition to more general cognitive impairments. They may also have difficulties in mobility, co-ordination and perception. Some pupils may use signs and symbols to support their communication and understanding. Their attainments may be within or below level 1 of the National Curriculum, or in the upper P scale range (P4–P8), for much of their school careers.

How can the subject teacher help?

- Liaise with parents.

- Arrange a work/subject buddy.

- Use visual supports: objects, pictures, symbols.

- Allow time to process information and formulate responses.

- Set differentiated tasks linked to the work of the rest of the class.

- Set achievable targets for each lesson or module of work.

- Accept different recording methods: drawings, audio or video recordings, photographs, etc.

- Give a series of short, varied activities within each lesson.

How can ICT help this group of pupils?

- Touch screens, rollerballs or switches may help them to access programs and navigate around the screen.

- Speech output means they can hear text.

- Symbols can help to record and read information.

- An overlay keyboard with pictures, and symbols can be used to open websites, etc.

- Multimedia may give more immediacy than text.

- Animations may make concepts come to life, e.g. caterpillar to butterfly and other metamorphoses.

Profound and multiple learning difficulties (PMLD)

Pupils with profound and multiple learning difficulties (PMLD) have complex learning needs. In addition to very severe learning difficulties, pupils have other significant difficulties, such as physical disabilities, sensory impairments or severe medical conditions. Pupils with PMLD require a high level of adult support, both for their learning needs and for their personal care.

They are able to access the curriculum through sensory experiences and stimulation. Some pupils communicate by gesture, eye pointing or symbols, others by very simple language. Their attainments are likely to remain in the early P scale range (P1–P4) throughout their school careers (that is below level 1 of the National Curriculum). The P scales provide small, achievable steps to monitor progress. Some pupils will make no progress or may even regress because of associated medical conditions. For this group, experiences are as important as attainment.

How can the subject teacher help?

- Liaise with parents and Teaching Assistants.

- Consider the classroom layout.

- Make it real – look, touch, hold.

- Use additional sensory supports: objects, pictures, fragrances, music, movements, food, etc.

- Take photographs to record experiences and responses.

- Set up a work/subject buddy rota for the class.

- Identify times when the pupil can work with groups.

How can ICT help this group of pupils?

- Touch screens, rollerballs or switches – use simple choice or cause and effect software.

- Speech output means they can hear text.

- Symbols can help to record and read information.

- An overlay keyboard with pictures, and symbols can be used to open websites, etc.

- Multimedia may give more immediacy than text.

- It can give access to a wider range of resources via the Internet than a school could provide for itself.

MENCAP, 117–123, Golden Lane, London EC1Y 0RT
Tel: 020 7454 0454 Website: http://www.mencap.org.uk

BEHAVIOURAL, EMOTIONAL AND SOCIAL DEVELOPMENT NEEDS

This term includes behavioural, emotional, and social difficulties and Attention Deficit Disorder with or without hyperactivity. These difficulties can be seen across the whole ability range and have a continuum of severity. Pupils with special educational needs in this category are those that have persistent difficulties despite an effective school behaviour policy and a personal and social curriculum.

Attention Deficit Disorder (with or without hyperactivity) (ADD/ADHD)

Attention Deficit Hyperactivity Disorder is a term used to describe children who exhibit over-active behaviour and impulsivity and who have difficulty in paying attention. It is caused by a form of brain dysfunction of a genetic nature. ADHD can sometimes be controlled effectively by medication. Children of all levels of ability can have ADHD.

Main characteristics:

- difficulty in following instructions and completing tasks
- easily distracted by noise, movement of others, objects attracting attention
- often doesn't listen when spoken to
- fidgets and becomes restless, can't sit still
- interferes with other pupils' work
- can't stop talking, interrupts others, calls out
- runs about when inappropriate
- has difficulty in waiting or taking turns
- acts impulsively without thinking about the consequences

How can the subject teacher help?

- Make eye contact and use the pupil's name when speaking to him.
- Keep instructions simple and visual.
- Give advanced warning when something is about to happen. Change or finish with a time, e.g. 'In two minutes I need you (pupil name) to . . .'

How can ICT help this group of pupils?

- CD-ROMs with sound, graphics and animations may grab attention in a way the teacher cannot.

- ICT is often very active and the kinaesthetic approach keeps pupils alert.

- With interactive whiteboards, the teacher can preload materials and activities to ensure variety.

ADD Information Services PO Box 340, Edgware, Middlesex, HA8 9HL
Tel: 020 8906 9068
ADDNET UK Website: www.btinternet.com/-black.ice/addnet/

Steve Y8 BESD

Steve thrives on attention. While he has lots of bright ideas, he can't work independently.

Skill: Exchanging and sharing information

Refining and presenting information: Use a digital camera to photograph basic ICT equipment and create an 'information sheet' using PowerPoint.

Steve will need to work with a TA when taking the photographs, but the attention and focus of the activity should help him concentrate. He should be made aware that placing plain card under items like the keyboard and mouse will produce better pictures.

Initial support with PowerPoint and instruction on inserting photographs and creating text boxes should lead to short periods of independent work.

It may be necessary to provide the equipment vocabulary and discuss how it is used. Steve should work towards producing a very visual presentation with some explanatory text. With support, the result will be something he is proud to show others.

(You can read more about Steven in Appendix 3.2.)

Behavioural, emotional and social difficulty (BESD)

Main characteristics:

- inattentive, poor concentration and lacks interest in school/school work

- easily frustrated, anxious about changes

- unable to work in groups

- unable to work independently, constantly seeking help

- confrontational – verbally aggressive towards pupils and/or adults

- physically aggressive towards pupils and/or adults

- destroys property – their own/ others

- appears withdrawn, distressed, unhappy, sulky, may self-harm

- lacks confidence, acts extremely frightened, lacks self-esteem

- finds it difficult to communicate

- finds it difficult to accept praise

How can the subject teacher help?

- Tell the pupil what you expect in advance, as regards work and behaviour.

- Check the ability level of the pupil. Some pupils are gifted but, if no one recognises this, they seek attention in other ways.

- Talk to the pupil to find out a bit about them.

- Consider the pupil's strengths and use them. Are they good with scanners? Cameras? Finding good music sites?

- Find and focus on some of their more likeable qualities.

- Focus your comments on the behaviour, not on the pupil, and offer an alternative way of behaving when correcting the pupil.

- Use 'please' and 'thank you' often.

- Be the guide and mentor rather than the authority figure at the front of the class. In the words of the old adage: 'the guide on the side, not the sage on the stage'.

How can ICT help this group of pupils?

- It is consistent. Don't laugh if you constantly have problems with your system!

- It can be good for record keeping – self-appraisal etc.

- Reward certificates can motivate.

- It removes some of the frustrating barriers to writing.

- It can support more creative work, e.g. music technology, presentations using multimedia.

- Writing frames can keep pupils on track.

COMMUNICATION AND INTERACTION NEEDS

Autistic Spectrum Disorders (ASD)

The term 'Autistic Spectrum Disorders' is used for a range of disorders affecting the development of social interaction, social communication and social imagination and flexibility of thought. This is known as the 'Triad of Impairments'. Pupils with ASD cover the full range of ability, and the severity of the impairment varies widely. Some pupils also have learning disabilities or other difficulties. Four times as many boys as girls are diagnosed with an ASD.

Main characteristics:

- **Social interaction**
  Pupils with an ASD find it difficult to understand social behaviour and this affects their ability to interact with children and adults. They do not always understand social contexts. They may experience high levels of stress and anxiety in settings that do not meet their needs or when routines are changed. This can lead to inappropriate behaviour.

- **Social communication**
  Understanding and use of non-verbal and verbal communication is impaired. Pupils with an ASD have difficulty understanding the communication of others and in developing effective communication themselves. They have a literal understanding of language. Many are delayed in learning to speak, and some never develop speech at all.

- **Social imagination and flexibility of thought**
  Pupils with an ASD have difficulty in thinking and behaving flexibly which may result in restricted, obsessional, or repetitive activities. They are often more interested in objects than people, and have intense interests in one particular area, such as trains or vacuum cleaners. Pupils work best when they have a routine. Unexpected changes in those routines will cause distress. Some pupils with Autistic Spectrum Disorders have a different perception of sounds, sights, smell, touch, and taste, and this can affect their response to these sensations.

Asperger's Syndrome

Asperger's Syndrome is a disorder at the able end of the autistic spectrum. People with Asperger Syndrome have average to high intelligence but share the same Triad of Impairments. They often want to make friends but do not understand the complex rules of social interaction. They have impaired fine and gross motor skills, with writing being a particular problem. Boys are more likely to be affected – with the ratio being 10:1 boys to girls. Because they appear 'odd' and naïve, these pupils are particularly vulnerable to bullying.

Main characteristics:

- **Social interaction**
  Pupils with Asperger's Syndrome want friends but have not developed the strategies necessary for making and sustaining friendships. They find it very difficult to learn social norms and to pick up on social cues. Highly social situations, such as lessons, can cause great anxiety.

- **Social communication**
  Pupils have appropriate spoken language but tend to sound formal and pedantic, using little expression and an unusual tone of voice. They have difficulty using and understanding non-verbal language, such as facial expression, gesture, body language and eye-contact. They have a literal understanding of language and do not grasp implied meanings.

- **Social imagination**
  Pupils with Asperger's Syndrome need structured environments, and routines they understand and can anticipate. They excel at learning facts and figures, but have difficulty understanding abstract concepts and in generalising information and skills. They often have all-consuming special interests.

How can the subject teacher help?

- Liaise with parents as they will have many useful strategies.

- Provide visual supports in class: objects, pictures, handouts, etc.

- Give a symbolic or written timetable for each day.

- Give advance warning of any changes to usual routines.

- Avoid using too much eye contact as it can cause distress.

- Give individual instructions using the pupil's name, e.g. 'Paul, bring me your book.'

- Avoid using metaphor, idiom or sarcasm – say what you mean in simple language.

- Provide additional visual cues in class.

- Give time to process questions and respond.

- Make sure pupils understand what to do.

- Allow alternatives to writing for recording.

- Use visual timetables and task activity lists.

- Prepare for changes to routines well in advance.

- Give written homework instructions and stick them into an exercise book.

- Have your own class rules and apply them consistently.

- Pupils may benefit from information presented using clear layout and language.

- Providing a framework at the beginning of any publication/presentation for the material's content (e.g. a flow diagram) can be helpful.

How can ICT help this group of pupils?

- It provides consistency whereas pupil interaction can be an unknown quantity.

- It might support and give a focus for social interaction and communication between two pupils working together.

- It can accommodate different learning styles.

- It lets pupils work at their own pace.

- It is non-judgmental and allows pupils more control of their learning.

- It can allow some pupils to be gainfully employed while the teacher works with others.

- It can motivate pupils to make a greater effort and can provide them with the extra practice required to master basic skills.

- It can give pupils instant feedback.

- It can provide pupils with a 'safe' environment to work in.

The National Autistic Society, 393 City Road, London EClV 1NG
Tel: 0845 070 4004 Helpline (10a.m.–4p.m., Mon–Fri) Tel: 020 7833 2299
Fax: 020 7833 9666
Email: nas@nas.org.uk Website: http://www.nas.org.uk

Semantic Pragmatic Disorder

Semantic Pragmatic Disorder is a communication disorder which falls within the autistic spectrum. 'Semantic' refers to the meanings of words and phrases and 'pragmatic' refers to the use of language in a social context. Pupils with this disorder have difficulties understanding the meaning of what people say and in using language to communicate effectively. Pupils with SPD find it difficult to extract the central meaning – saliency – of situations.

Main characteristics:

- delayed language development

- fluent speech but may sound stilted or over-formal

- may repeat phrases out of context from videos or adult conversations

- difficulty understanding abstract concepts

- limited or inappropriate use of eye contact, facial expression or gesture

- motor skills problems

How can the subject teacher help?

- Sit the pupil at the front of the room to avoid distractions.

- Use visual supports: objects, pictures, symbols.

- Pair with a work/subject buddy.

- Create a calm working environment with clear classroom rules.

- Be specific and unambiguous when giving instructions.

- Make sure instructions are understood, especially when using subject-specific vocabulary that can have another meaning in a different context.

How can ICT help this group of pupils?

- There are lots of rewards, e.g. software which gives feedback (some pupils talk to the software).

- CD-ROMs with hyperlinks mean information is structured and more detail or definitions are off screen.

- Story boarding can help to develop ideas and language.

- Writing frames can keep pupils on track.

- Clicker and personal or topic dictionaries can relieve stress and keep pupils focused on the language they need for a particular class.

AFASIC, 2nd Floor, 50–52 Great Sutton Street, London EC1V 0DJ
Tel: 0845 355 5577 (Helpline 11a.m.–2p.m.) Tel: 020 7490 9410 Fax: 020 7251 2834
Email: info@afasic.org.uk Website: http://www.afasic.org.uk

Susan Y10

Susan has been variously labelled as having Asperger's and 'cocktail party syndrome'. Her language is sometimes quite sophisticated, but her understanding and ability to use language for school work operate at a much lower level. She is poor at turn taking and shouts out in class.

Skill: Developing ideas and making things happen

Models and modelling: Use a spreadsheet to explore the cost of feeding different animals in a zoo.

Susan will need clear instructions and worked examples to help her understand the concept of modelling. Prepare a spreadsheet with large cells and insert pictures of three different animals in the first column, perhaps an elephant, a monkey and a fish. In the next column insert pictures of the daily food consumption for each animal.

    This can be followed by columns for variables, such as the number of animals and daily food costs. Other columns could calculate weekly and yearly food costs and total food budget. With support, Susan can compare the food budget for different combinations of animals in the zoo and find the answers to simple 'what if?' questions. The next stage would be for Susan to create a similar 'visual' spreadsheet model herself.

(You can read more about Susan in Appendix 3.2.)

Speech, language and communication difficulties (SLCD)

Pupils with speech, language and communication difficulties have problems understanding what others say and/or making others understand what they say. Their development of speech and language skills may be significantly delayed. Speech and language difficulties are very common in young children but most problems are resolved during the primary years. Problems that persist beyond the transfer to secondary school will be more severe. Any problem affecting speech, language and communication will have a significant effect on a pupil's self-esteem, and personal and social relationships. The development of literacy skills is also likely to be affected. Even where pupils learn to decode, they may not understand what they have read. Sign language gives pupils an additional method of communication. Pupils with speech, language and communication difficulties cover the whole range of academic abilities.

Main characteristics:

- **Speech difficulties**
  Pupils who have difficulties with expressive language may experience problems in articulation and the production of speech sounds, or in co-ordinating the muscles that control speech. They may have a stammer or some other form of dysfluency

- **Language/communication difficulties**
  Pupils with receptive language impairments have difficulty understanding the meaning of what others say. They may use words incorrectly with inappropriate grammatical patterns, have a reduced vocabulary, or find it hard to recall words and express ideas. Some pupils will also have difficulty using and understanding eye-contact, facial expression, gesture and body language.

How can the subject teacher help?

- Talk to parents, speech therapist – and the pupil.

- Learn the most common signs for your subject.

- Use visual supports: objects, pictures, symbols.

- Use the pupil's name when addressing them.

- Give one instruction at a time, using short, simple sentences.

- Give time to respond before repeating a question.

- Make sure pupils understand what they have to do before starting a task.

- Pair with a work/subject buddy.

- Give written homework instructions.

How can ICT help this group of pupils?

- It improves presentation.

- Clip art and other visual clues can help pupils target information.

- It gives access to vocabulary.

- Speech feedback is not so dependent on reading skills.

ICAN4 Dyer's Buildings, Holborn, London EC1N 2QP
Tel: 0845 225 4071
Email: info@ican.org.uk Website: http://www.ican.org.uk
AFASIC 2nd Floor, 50–52, Great Sutton Street, London EC1V 0DJ
Tel: 0845 355 5577 (Helpline) Tel: 020 7490 9410 Fax: 020 7251 2834
Email: info@afasic.org.uk Website: http://www.afasic.org.uk

Tourette's Syndrome (TS)

Tourette's Syndrome is a neurological disorder characterised by tics. Tics are involuntary rapid or sudden movements or sounds that are frequently repeated. There is a wide range of severity of the condition with some people having no need to seek medical help whilst others have a socially disabling condition. The tics can be suppressed for a short time but will be more noticeable when the pupil is anxious or excited.

Main characteristics:

Physical tics
Physical tics range from simple blinking or nodding through more complex movements to more extreme conditions such as echopraxia (imitating actions seen) or copropraxia (repeatedly making obscene gestures).

Vocal tics
Vocal tics may be as simple as throat clearing or coughing but can progress to be as extreme as echolalia (the repetition of what was last heard) or coprolalia (the repetition of obscene words).

TS itself causes no behavioural or educational problems but other, associated disorders such as Attention Deficit Hyperactivity Disorder (ADHD) or Obsessive Compulsive Disorder (OCD) may be present.

How can the subject teacher help?

- Establish a rapport with the pupil.
- Talk to the parents.
- Agree an 'escape route' signal should the tics become disruptive.
- Allow the pupil to sit at the back of the room to prevent staring.
- Give access to a computer to reduce handwriting.
- Make sure the pupil is not teased or bullied.
- Be alert for signs of anxiety or depression.

How can ICT help this group of pupils?

- It improves presentation.
- Clip art and other visual clues can help them target information.
- Can be good for self-appraisal, etc.

- It removes some of the frustrations and lets pupils produce work.

- It can support more creative work such as art, media, video, music.

- Writing frames and outlines can keep pupils on track.

Tourette Syndrome (UK) Association
PO Box 26149, Dunfermline, KY12 7YU
Tel: 0845 458 1252 (Helpline) Tel: 01383 629600 (Admin)
Fax: 01383 629609
Email: enquiries@tsa.org.uk Website: http://www.tsa.org.uk

SENSORY AND/OR PHYSICAL NEEDS

Cerebral palsy (CP)

Cerebral palsy is a persistent disorder of movement and posture. It is caused by damage or lack of development to part of the brain before or during birth or in early childhood. Problems vary from slight clumsiness to more severe lack of control of movements. Pupils with CP may also have learning difficulties. They may use a wheelchair or other mobility aid.

Main characteristics:

There are three main forms of cerebral palsy:

- *spasticity* – disordered control of movement associated with stiffened muscles

- *athetosis* – frequent involuntary movements

- *ataxia* – an unsteady gait with balance difficulties and poor spatial awareness

Pupils may also have communication difficulties.

How can the subject teacher help?

- Talk to parents, the physiotherapist – and the pupil.

- Consider the classroom layout.

- Have high academic expectations.

- Use visual supports: objects, pictures, symbols.

- Arrange a work/subject buddy.

- Speak directly to the pupil rather than through a Teaching Assistant.

- Ensure access to appropriate IT equipment for the subject – and that it is used.

- Government initiatives such as the CAP Project http://cap.becta.org.uk/ may offer access to additional equipment.

- Try to ensure the same technology is used at home and school.

How can ICT help this group of pupils?

- It may literally give them a voice.

- It may be their only means of communication.

- It may augment or support spoken or written communication.

- Speech recognition technology may help them to write and produce work even though they may lack physical stamina and tire easily.

- Switches can be used with spreadsheets, PowerPoint or other standard software which is used in the ICT curriculum.

Scope, PO Box 833, Milton Keynes, MK12 5NY
Tel: 0808 800 3333 (Freephone helpline) Fax: 01908 321051
Email: cphelpline@scope.org.uk Website: http://www.scope.org.uk

---

Physical disability (PD)

There is a wide range of physical disabilities, and pupils with PD cover all academic abilities. Some pupils are able to access the curriculum and learn effectively without additional educational provision. They have a disability but do not have a special educational need. For other pupils, the impact on their education may be severe, and the school will need to make adjustments to enable them to access the curriculum.

Some pupils with a physical disability have associated medical conditions which may impact on their mobility. These include cerebral palsy, heart disease, spina bifida and hydrocephalus, and muscular dystrophy. Pupils with physical disabilities may also have sensory impairments, neurological problems, or learning difficulties. They may use a wheelchair and/or additional mobility aids. Some pupils will be mobile but may have significant fine motor difficulties which require support. Others may need augmentative or alternative communication aids.

Pupils with a physical disability may need to miss lessons to attend physiotherapy or medical appointments. They are also likely to become very tired as they expend greater effort to complete everyday tasks. Schools will need to be flexible and sensitive to individual pupil needs.

How can the subject teacher help?

- Get to know pupils and parents and they will help you make the right adjustments.

- Maintain high expectations.

- Consider the classroom layout.

- Allow the pupil to leave lessons a few minutes early to avoid busy corridors and give time to get to the next lesson.

- Set homework earlier in the lesson so instructions are not missed.

- Speak directly to the pupil rather than through a Teaching Assistant.

- Let pupils make their own decisions.

- Ensure access to appropriate IT equipment for the lesson – and that it is used!

- Give alternative ways of recording work.

- Plan to cover work missed through medical or physiotherapy appointments.

- Be sensitive to fatigue, especially at the end of the school day.

How can ICT help this group of pupils?

- You can alter the setting on the computer to accommodate some of their access problems. Internet information is often easier to access than information from a book where they have to turn pages or use an index, etc.

- The search facility helps them locate information easily.

- Switches may give access where other input devices fail.

- Keyboarding is easier than writing.

- A Key guard ensures more accurate typing.

- A Trackerball or joystick makes navigation easier.

Hearing impairment (HI)

The term 'hearing impairment' is a generic term used to describe all hearing loss. The main types of loss are monaural, conductive, sensory and mixed loss. The degree of hearing loss is described as mild, moderate, severe or profound. Some children rely on lip reading, others will use hearing aids, and a small proportion will have British Sign Language (BSL) as their primary means of communication.

How can the subject teacher help?

- Check the degree of loss the pupil has.

- Check the best seating position (e.g. away from the hum of OHP, computers, with good ear to speaker).

- Check that the pupil can see your face for facial expressions and lip reading.

- Provide a list of vocabulary, context and visual clues, especially for new subjects.

- During class discussion, allow one pupil to speak at a time and indicate where the speaker is.

- Check that any aids are working and if there is any other specialist equipment available.

- Make sure that the light falls on your face and lips. Do not stand with your back to a window.

- If you use interactive whiteboards, ensure that the beam does not prevent the pupil from seeing your face.

- Ban small talk.

How can ICT help this group of pupils?

- It is easy to modify and differentiate language in worksheets.

- You can include clip art etc. to reinforce or clarify meaning.

- It gives help with sequencing/story telling/narrative structures.

- There are visual clues and information on screen.

- Pupils can communicate at a distance without being disadvantaged.

- Email etc. motivates pupils using BSL to communicate in their second language (English).

Kuli Profound hearing loss

Kuli finds it quite hard to get the full message from text alone and has particular problems with new vocabulary.

Skill: Finding things out

Searching and selecting: Use the Internet to search for clip art to be used in the creation of a vocabulary information sheet.

Kuli will benefit from a logical, focused approach to searching the Internet. Show him a simple information sheet that has been created in PowerPoint using clipart to illustrate verbs. His task will be to search the Internet to find similar images and create his own sheet (the creation of the worksheet could be developed in his sessions with the teacher of the deaf).

A visual, step-by-step guide to searching the Internet would help Kuli a great deal in the initial stages. If this is created using PowerPoint it can be printed out as a booklet or Kuli can work through it on screen. The onscreen version can also contain links to web pages that will control and focus the search at first and then encourage the use of a search engine.

(You can read more about Kuli in Appendix 3.2.)

Royal Institute for the Deaf (RNID), 19–23 Featherstone Street,
London EC1Y 8SL
Tel: 0808 808 0123
British Deaf Association (BDA) 1–3 Worship Street, London ECZA 2AB
British Association of Teachers of the Deaf (BATOD), The Orchard, Leven,
North Humberside, HU17 5QA
Website: www.batod.org.uk

Visual impairment (VI)

Visual impairment refers to a range of difficulties, including those pupils with monocular vision (vision in one eye), those who are partially sighted and those who are blind. Pupils with visual impairment cover the whole ability range and some pupils may have other SEN.

How can the subject teacher help?

- Check the optimum position for the pupil, e.g. for a monocular pupil, their good eye should be towards the action.

- Always provide the pupil with their own copy of the text.

- Provide enlarged print copies of written text.

- Check use of ICT (enlarged icons, talking text, teach keyboard skills).

- Do not stand with your back to the window as this creates a silhouette and makes it harder for the pupil to see you.

- Draw the pupil's attention to displays – which they may not notice.

- Make sure the floor is kept free of clutter.

- Tell the pupil if there is a change to the layout of a space.

- Ask if there is any specialist equipment available (enlarged print dictionaries, lights, talking scales).

How can ICT help this group of pupils?

- The Internet is a good source of information and can be accessed via a screen reader.

- A Web cam can enlarge small details on a laptop screen and make them visible.

- Speech feedback can be used to proofread work.

- Touch typing is easier than hand writing.

- You can change text to a large font easily.

- You can change screen colours for greater legibility.

Royal National Institute of the Blind (RNIB), 105 Judd Street, London, WC1H 9NE
Tel: 020 7388 1266 Fax: 020 7388 2034
See also http://www.svtc.org.uk/resources/sen/sen30.pdf

Multi-sensory impairment

Pupils with multi-sensory impairment have a combination of visual and hearing difficulties. They may also have other additional disabilities that make their situation complex. A pupil with these difficulties is likely to have a high level of individual support.

How can the subject teacher help?

- The subject teacher will need to liaise with support staff to ascertain the appropriate provision within each subject.

- Consideration will need to be given to alternative means of communication.

- Be prepared to be flexible and to adapt tasks, targets and assessment procedures.

How can ICT help this group of pupils?

- It enables them to communicate at a distance on an equal par with anyone else.

- It can be the only way of getting access to any information they choose, instead of only having information which others choose to give them.

CHAPTER 4

The Inclusive Classroom

ICT has a lot of equipment! When people talk about ICT, it conjures up images of computer rooms and networks, of whiteboards and data projection panels, of robots and control technology. Increasingly we are moving to wireless networks, laptops, palm tops, digital cameras and 'anywhere, any place, any time' technology. However, teachers need to think about the physical design of the classroom in order to manage effectively large quantities of equipment.

> Greenwich Millennium Primary School and Health Centre is one prototype for the 'classroom of the future':
>
> Each classroom at MPS is equipped with multiple network points, an interactive whiteboard and other digital technologies such as digital cameras and web cameras. The building is designed to be light and airy to provide an optimum working environment; clever features such as automatic blinds on the windows, to reduce light levels on bright days, are commonplace.[1]

While not all teachers will be working in a brand new school, there are some changes which can be made to improve your facilities. Consider your classroom:

- Does the layout support or restrict good ICT provision?

- Is there room for all pupils to work at computers with papers etc. beside the keyboards?

- Can the teacher walk round and easily see what each pupil is doing?

- Can the teacher demonstrate work on a computer screen to the whole class?

Furniture

In practice, computer rooms are rarely beacons of high-tech excellence. If you look round the average computer classroom, you will see monitors which are stacked on top of bases on trolleys so pupils have to crane their necks upwards. Often scanners and printers have been put in as an afterthought, tucked away in a corner or even in the corridor outside. Tables and chairs matter too. Do you have any height-adjustable trolleys or is everything fixed? There might be a cheap and cheerful solution such as a booster cushion for someone who is very small and cannot get close enough to the monitor. Sometimes a pupil needs a special chair for extra comfort and support, but obviously it will not be feasible to have such furniture in every room.

The trouble is that schools buy 'job lots' of furniture. It is not uncommon to see a computer room entirely full of swivel chairs. This looks neat and the chairs move easily. In fact, they move too easily. Some pupils need to lean on the back of a chair for support, and a chair which rolls away is not stable enough for them. Also there is a whole group of children in any class who will spend a lot of the lesson spinning round or having chair races. Some people need arms on the chair to support their own arms, especially as they get tired and need a rest from keyboarding. Others find the arms an impediment which stops them getting close enough to the monitor. A partially sighted pupil may need to be just a couple of inches away to see the screen. The general rule is to have a variety of chairs in the room. Don't go for the cosmetic approach of choosing furniture for its looks. A mixed economy is the best approach to meet the needs of pupils who, after all, come in all shapes and sizes.

The position of the monitor is also crucial. Computer vision syndrome is becoming as common as repetitive strain injury (RSI). Symptoms include sore, dry eyes, headaches and blurred vision. Computers should ideally be at 90 degrees to a light source. You should be looking downwards onto the monitor, and it should be about 60 cm away from your eyes.

Whiteboards

Whiteboards may be a good option for training pupils in the use of ICT packages, and enable all pupils to learn about them simultaneously. This approach allows for easy intervention by a signer or Classroom Assistant.

Using an ordinary whiteboard with a computer and data projector has many advantages – it's cheap, quick to set up and can be used with dry marker pens. It can be used in a blended learning way combining traditional and e-learning techniques. If used with a wireless tablet, like the Interwrite Schoolpad, an ordinary whiteboard can become almost as versatile as an interactive whiteboard. The wireless tablet communicates with the computer and can be passed round the classroom, allowing pupils to add written comments and sketches which appear on the whiteboard. The tablet also gives complete control of the computer in the same way as a laptop touchpad does. It is a great solution for pupils with mobility problems who can't get to the board easily to make contributions to the lesson, and ideal in any situation where movement around the room needs to be kept to a minimum.

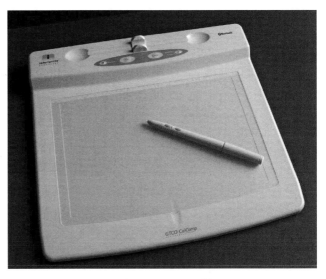

Wireless Interwrite tablet

The whiteboard data projector set-up is a simple and effective way to demonstrate techniques and introduce new topics. This method of delivery will help focus pupils' attention, ensure good eye contact and provide the conditions for good pupil/teacher interaction.

Interactive whiteboards

Interactive whiteboards are very much the teaching technology of the moment. You could be forgiven for thinking that it is impossible to teach without access to this technology. Certainly there are many advantages:

- It is easier to integrate sound and video as part of the lesson. This can more clearly demonstrate the relationship between the written word and what is heard.

- Colour and pictures reach out to a wider range of learning styles, so those who are visual learners can benefit greatly.

- The printout facility can help to reinforce messages. Printouts are especially useful for pupils with dyslexia, who copy slowly and inaccurately and may have short-term memory problems.

- Electronic copies can be made of both the initial presentation and the notes and comments generated in the lesson. This could be helpful for TAs supporting pupils before and after a session.

- Pupils can make written contributions. They can sort, collect and group images and demonstrate to the whole group. A wireless tablet can also be used with an interactive whiteboard (see above).

However, whiteboards are not a universal remedy for all pupils. There are a number of issues which affect pupils with special needs, not least health and safety.

(For more information on the health and safety issues see Appendix 2.4.) Research[2] suggests that the whiteboard leads to a faster pace of lesson and this may not suit those who need time for ideas and vocabulary to sink in.

The interactive whiteboard may also dictate the layout of the room. Classrooms are not designed for an interactive whiteboard so it may not be well sited. To use it effectively and not stand in its beam, you will need a clear space either side. Too often this area is taken up by cupboards so that the teacher is either reaching over or causing shadow to fall on the screen, or obscuring the view by standing in the way. Lighting is another issue. Becta advises that 'interactive whiteboards can be very difficult to see when direct sunlight shines on them. If a board is in direct sunlight at any time of the school day, black-out blinds (or similar) will be needed.'[3] You need to be sure that all pupils can see the board and that a child with a visual impairment is not being dazzled.

Organising the layout of the ICT room

The majority of computer rooms were not purpose built and often just evolved. Sometimes the room is so overcrowded that the door will not open to its full extent, making ingress difficult, not just for the child in a wheelchair but for anyone using a walking frame. Think about how pupils will get around the room. Children with poor motor control, such as pupils with dyspraxia, need clear spaces to walk around in. What happens to bags and coats in the ICT rooms? Are there pegs provided, or alternative cupboard space?

Think about the layout of the equipment in the room. The layout of an ICT room is always important for any teaching situation but especially so when considering the needs of pupils with SEN. Clear, unobstructed access into and around the room is vital for those with mobility challenges or for wheelchair users. It is also essential that all users can evacuate the room safely in an emergency.

These considerations have to be balanced against the need for some pupils to be close to the teacher or whiteboard to enable them to see adequately or to have good eye contact and a clear view of the teacher's face to facilitate lip reading. It may also be necessary to work with a communication support assistant who provides sign language support when needed. The room layout should cater for this in whole-class demonstration situations as well as for one-to-one support. Installing an interactive whiteboard in a classroom is often a compromise, but ideally it should be sited to allow the teacher to work from either side and be able to stand clear of the board to avoid casting a shadow. Data projectors should be ceiling mounted to avoid glare and minimise shadows. It is worth noting that wheelchair users may find the beam from a table-mounted projector shines directly in their eyes. This is a situation that must be avoided for all pupils.

An area where the pupils can be grouped in a 'u' or horseshoe shape for class discussions or demonstrations will improve access for pupils with visual and hearing impairments. This is particularly important in large rooms where computers are arranged around the edge, or in rooms where computers are in rows or clusters and the lack of a direct sight line makes interaction difficult.

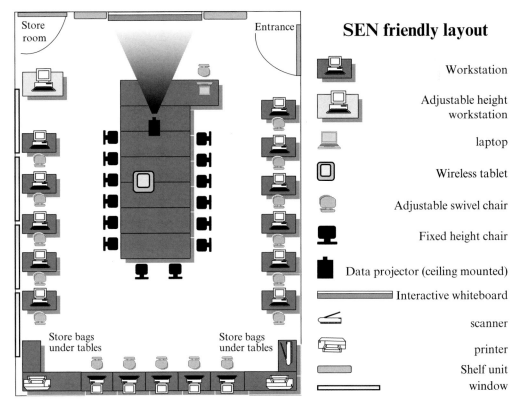

SEN friendly classroom

Points to note:

- unobstructed entrance into the room

- clear access around room

- storage for bags

- some stable, fixed-height chairs

- adjustable height workstation

- screens at right angle to windows

- clear view of the whiteboard and teacher

- space at each side of the whiteboard for the teacher to stand

- horseshoe arrangement for demonstrations and discussions

- ceiling-mounted data projector

- interactive whiteboard at a suitable height

- a wireless tablet to allow all to contribute to the lesson

(For more about ICT room layout look at this document on the Becta website: http://buildingthegrid.becta.org.uk/docs/ict_design.pdf)

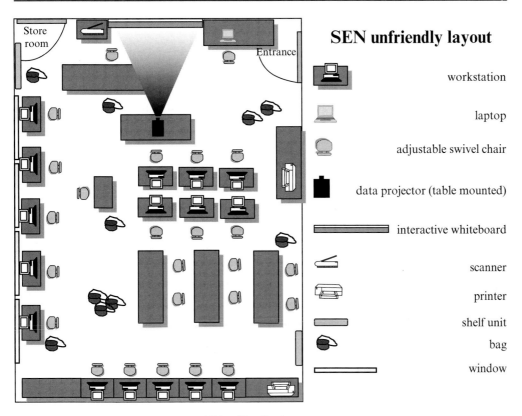

SEN unfriendly classroom

Improving accessibility

There are many ways of increasing physical access to a computer and you will find details of accessibility options within the computer in Appendix 4.1. It is tempting to thumb through catalogues looking for pieces of equipment – enlarged keyboards, joysticks etc. – which will meet the needs of individual pupils with disabilities. However, some accessibility equipment can open up the world of ICT to a whole range of learners. You don't need to have a physical disability to need a bit of extra support. What about the child with ME or who has glandular fever or just tires easily? People who have dyslexia or are long sighted might benefit from large print or changing screen colours. Pupils need to:

- navigate
- select and move an object
- input text

Navigate

Most of us probably use a mouse to get around a screen and open menus. The most popular mouse alternatives are a rollerball or a trackerball. Some have colour-coded buttons, including a draglock, which means that the cursor can only go up and down the screen or left to right. This is good for someone with shaky, erratic movements or indeed for someone who has problems doing two things at once.

Many children who have moved from special schools into mainstream will be used to having such equipment readily available. Joysticks are another solution. They have an 'arcade game' image to them, but there are some which work well with standard applications such as word processing. Joysticks are generally robust and users adapt to them quite quickly. A wheel mouse is universally useful for scrolling and browsing and may be particularly helpful for certain pupils.

Number pad

MS Windows allows the number keys on the standard keyboard to be used for mouse control. The mouse pointer can be moved from side to side and up and down at the press of a key. This is particularly useful for those who find holding a conventional mouse difficult. This can be used to select items, open folders and programs and display the drop-down menus usually associated with a right mouse click. It cannot be used to click and drag to move objects. (See Appendix 4.1 for more details.)

Overlays

Concept keyboards, overlay keyboards or Intellikeys – they are known by different names but essentially they are a flat plug-in accessory for use with overlays. These overlays can be for anything – they might emulate a mouse or switches. Tactile overlays are good for pupils with a visual impairment. They work well for people with cognitive difficulties too. They can be programmed so that when you press or hit part of the board, an application will open such as email, or it will take you to favourite websites. This can be good for people who would get frustrated by typing in an enormous URL to reach a website. They may also be used to input text, but there are better options for this for many of the pupils you will encounter in mainstream.

Intellikeys

Switches

Pupils who have difficulty using a conventional keyboard, mouse or any of the mouse alternatives may find a switch control system helpful. Switches can be connected to the computer in place of, or as well as, a mouse. A switch is usually a small, rounded disc that is operated by a single touch, and can be adjusted to activate by a very light touch or a heavy thump. The switch works in conjunction with software which scans objects on the screen, highlighting each in turn. As this cycle of highlighting progresses, the user can select an object by touching the switch when the desired object is highlighted.

Pictures, words and even individual letters from an on-screen keyboard can be selected in this way, allowing the user to build up a document or complete multiple-choice tasks.

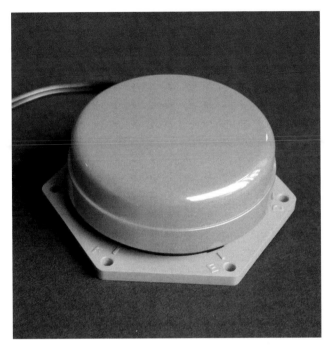

Switch

A software program that integrates well with switches is Clicker. This program allows the teacher to create and tailor materials to suit pupils' needs and enables pupils to create text and image documents with and without the use of switches.

Select and move an object

A mouse click to select an object and a click and drag to move an object are common tasks for all computer users. Pupils who have difficulty with fine motor skill tasks may find these combination activities impossible. Some of the equipment mentioned in the Navigate section will assist with selecting and moving activities.

Roisin

Roisin broke her right arm and was unable to use a pen. She used her left hand to type in text but this was very slow. She used smartNAV. This controlled the pointer on screen by tracking a reflective dot that she put on her forehead. She used a predictive word-processing package which meant that once she had typed the first one or two letters, a list of suggestions appeared on screen. She went from about 40 letters per minute to about 25 words.

Trackerball and joystick

Choose one that has a click-lock button so the pointer can be positioned over the object, the hand removed to press the lock button and the object dragged into place. The lock button is then pressed again to release the lock. The trackerball and joystick are the favoured option for selecting and moving tasks.

Trackerball

Graphics tablet

This uses a stylus to move the mouse pointer and with careful location and fixing of the tablet may be a solution for some pupils. Selection and click and drag functions can be carried out with the stylus.

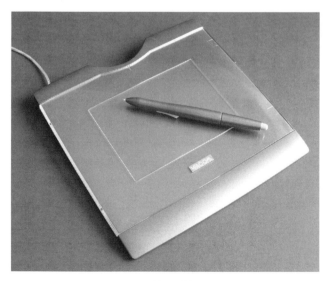

Graphics tablet

Inputting

Keyboards and key guards

These come in all shapes and sizes and one size does not necessarily fit all. If we are going to encourage pupils to touch type – and it certainly is advisable for learners with hearing loss who need to focus on all visual clues – then we need a keyboard which is not too big and not too little, but just right. How about a small keyboard for little hands? However, the learner with dyspraxia may tend to thump when typing, so a big keyboard is better for the heavy handed!

Wrist rests will help a whole range of people – including staff – and help to prevent repetitive strain injury (RSI).

If you have a pupil with poor motor skills think about a key guard. A tremor is one of the occasional side effects of Ritalin, prescribed to many children with Attention Deficit Hyperactivity Disorder. Imagine the frustration of hitting a key and seeing a whole row of letters appear. A key guard is a plastic or metal cover that fits over the top of the keyboard so that the pupil has to poke the key through the hole. Always buy the guard at the same time as you purchase the keyboard to ensure a proper fit. Remember, manufacturers change the design of a keyboard very regularly and a key guard which is a less than perfect fit is of no use at all.

Big Keys

Stickers

If you don't want to buy a range of keyboards, think about changing the response rate on the Microsoft accessibility options (see Appendix 4.1) and buying stickers or a keyboard cover. Changing the colours can make it easier to find your way round a keyboard. Keytop stickers come in a variety of colour combinations. They can be black text on yellow, white text on black or black text on white, and are available as upper or lower case sets.

Plastic keyboard covers fasten over a standard keyboard with Velcro. These covers can be a good alternative to stickers as they come in high contrast format or lower case. They are also waterproof so may be a good choice in other areas of the school, e.g. science labs, art rooms, or if pupils are likely to dribble onto the keyboard. You will have seen them in use in garages and other 'dirty areas' where they protect the keyboard from oil and grime. Of course, these options will not meet the needs of people who find a keyboard too big!

Voice recognition

This is another input device which has both fans and critics! It is often seen as a solution for pupils with dyslexia who read and speak better than they write, but speech input requires quite high level skills. Dictation is an art form in itself, and many young learners are embarrassed at being overheard. The user must also be able to check the accuracy of the text to see if the system has translated the sounds into the right words. This necessitates good reading skills. There are also issues about background noise. Nevertheless, for some learners this is an excellent medium for getting their thoughts on paper.

Assistive writing packages

These might include predictive word-processing packages such as *PenFriend, Co: Writer* or *TextHelp* where you type the first letter and the software suggests suitable words. For many learners, it is an effort to recall spellings. As a result they end up operating at letter and single word level and they get muddled and lose track of what they are saying. Once input speeds up, the quality of their work improves dramatically. Similarly, programs such as *Clicker* and *WordBar* with their on-screen topic wordlists, personal dictionaries or phrase banks can have a startling impact on output. They provide more than a list of words: they somehow act as an aide memoire too. Some pupils benefit from planning tools or writing frames. Others will need a symbol word processor to produce written evidence of their capabilities.

PowerPoint

Lots of teachers use PowerPoint for whole-class presentations and there are many advantages:

- It's visual.

- Animations can help to explain concepts.

- It is easy to incorporate sound and video clips.

- It looks professional.

Harry Y7 Dyslexia

Harry is a very anxious little boy and although he has now started at secondary school, he still seems to be a 'little boy'. His parents have been very concerned about his slow progress in reading and writing and arranged for a dyslexia assessment when he was eight years old. They also employ a private tutor who comes to the house for two hours per week and they spend time each evening and at weekends hearing him read and working on phonics with him.

Harry finds it hard to get his ideas down on paper. Not only does he have spelling problems but he often leaves words out and his work frequently does not make sense. In primary school, he had an amanuensis but this was a disaster because he did not always have the same person, so they never developed a way of working together, and he felt he was always under pressure.

In secondary school, he is being helped to become more independent and to explore a range of technology. Staff are looking at input devices so he can get his ideas on paper. He is using voice recognition technology which lets him produce work without worrying how to write and spell. His English teacher has already noticed an improvement in his spelling. 'Before using *Via Voice Gold*, Harry would often write (and therefore see) six or seven different spellings of one word, so he never had any sense of the correct shape of a word or common letter strings. With voice recognition, every word is correctly spelt. As Harry is only seeing correct spellings, his sense of what a word should look like is also improving.'

Like many other pupils with dyslexia, Harry also has problems in organising his thoughts. The school is beginning to experiment with *StarThink* a 'mind-mapping' program from the makers of *StarSpell*, which Harry used a lot in primary school. It's early days yet, but there are signs that he is thinking more fluently and capturing his ideas on paper.

The SENCO and the ICT co-ordinator are now beginning to address the issue of worksheets. Most teachers get pupils to fill in worksheets, but pupils with handwriting problems are at a disadvantage. They cannot show what they can do and often cannot read their own work, so it is no use for revision. The school now expects all staff to provide electronic versions of worksheets. These can be used by all pupils who need computer support. In time, these will be lodged on an intranet, but for the time being they are kept on discs with the TA.

(You can read more about Harry in Appendix 3.2)

- You can annotate the slide with extra arrows etc. on a whiteboard or interactive whiteboard.

- If an interactive whiteboard with Internet access is available, web page links in PowerPoint are an efficient way to broaden the scope of a lesson and regain flagging concentration.

We know all the pros, but what about the cons? We have all sat through PowerPoint presentations where the speaker has filled slides with too much text. The colour combinations probably looked good on the computer at home but are hard to read once projected. The medium dominates the message: it is used in a linear fashion and the teacher can only go backwards or forwards and not go off at a tangent to help learners.

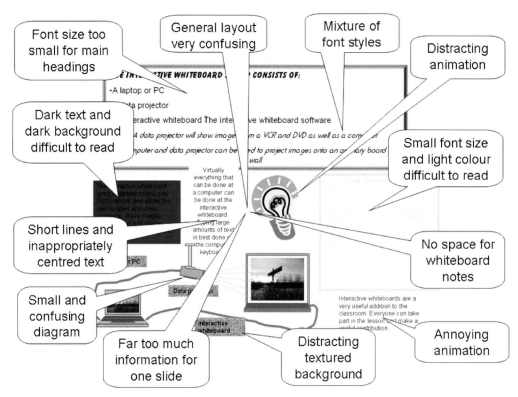

An example of a PowerPoint slide that could be confusing to pupils.

Try using branching templates or hyperlinks to jump to slides providing additional information to be shown when needed. You will find examples called 'Making Tea & Coffee' and 'Flowers & Leaves', as well as various templates and more information on good and bad PowerPoint slides on the accompanying CD-ROM.

Guidelines for legibility

- Do not cram in too much information.

- Use two or three slides rather than one to get the point across.

- Select background colours carefully – pastel shades are best.

- Choose 24 point Arial for font.

- Lay out nicely with illustrations.

Many of the same guidelines apply to print materials as well. Teachers often worry about having 24 slides for a PowerPoint and then try to cut out some of the information.

Improving access to the Web

Although the Web is a great source of information, some people find it takes too long to scan through all the references. Set up a document or Clicker grid with favourites to help pupils who are likely to type in an address very slowly or get

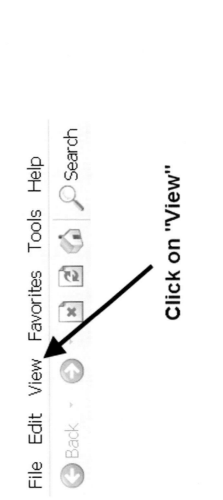

David Fulton Publishers - Microsoft Internet Explorer

File   Edit   View   Favorites   Tools   Help

Back ▾   ⏹ ✕ 🔄 🏠   🔍 Search   ⭐ Favorites   ⏱

Address 🔗 http://www.fultonpublishers.co.uk/

Open your Internet Explorer

File   Edit   View   Favorites   Tools   Help

Back ▾   ⏹ ✕ 🔄 🏠   🔍 Search

Click on "View"

Toolbars		▸
✓ Status Bar		▸
Explorer Bar		▸
Go To		▸
Stop	Esc	
Refresh	F5	
Text Size		▸
Encoding		▸
Source		
Privacy Report...		
Full Screen	F11	

Largest
Larger
• Medium
Smaller
Smallest

Click on "Text Size" and choose a suitable font size

Internet text size

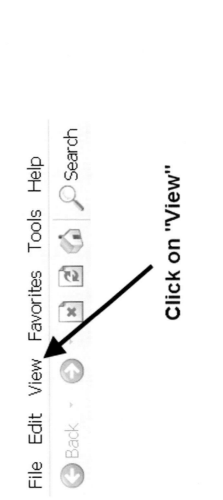

some of the string of letters in the wrong order. You can also increase the readability of the Internet by playing with the display settings. Often we just use the default settings, but if you go to the View menu – text – and change it from medium to large it projects better.

References

[1] 'An exploration of the use of ICT at the Millennium Primary School, Greenwich': http://www.becta.org.uk/research

[2] Becta guidance: 'VTC – Whiteboards and Modern Foreign Languages': curriculum.becta.org.uk/docserver.php?docid=5006

[3] See Becta guidance: 'Planning to purchase an interactive whiteboard': http://www.becta.org.uk/ntss/ntss.cfm?id=3160

Useful contacts

ACE Centre Advisory Trust – www.ace-centre.org.uk
ACE Centre North – www.ace-north.org.uk
Becta – www.becta.org.uk
CALL Centre – callcentre.education.ed.ac.uk
Microsoft Accessibility – www.microsoft.com/enable/

Useful documents

Disability Rights Commission: http://www.drc-gb.org/drc/default.asp
Education Act 1996 – Special Educational Needs (SEN) provisions: http://www.hmso.gov.uk/acts/acts1996/96056-zd.htm#p4c1
Special Educational Needs and Disability Act 2001: http://www.hmso.gov.uk/acts/acts2001/20010010.htm
SEN and Disability Tribunal: http://www.sentribunal.gov.uk/index.cfm
World Wide Web Consortium (W3C) – Web Content Accessibility Guidelines: http://www.w3.org/TR/WAI-WEBCONTENT/

Teaching and Learning Styles

An inclusive classroom is very hard to define but it is about meeting all individual needs through appropriate support and adaptation of the curriculum.

Teachers themselves are, of course, key components in an inclusive approach to curriculum delivery. There are still relatively few teachers who trained to teach ICT as their main subject. Some are enthusiasts who are excited by the technology, and who keep up to date by reading magazines and trawling the Internet. They are confident users who like the challenge of new technology. If they don't know something, they will find it out. However, there are many other teachers for whom ICT is very much a second string to their bow. They can work through the ICT syllabus but like to be in charge, in case something goes wrong. Similarly, Teaching Assistants (whose role will be covered in more depth in Chapter 7) are not necessarily confident users. As a result, there are many staff who feel vulnerable: they lack the confidence to take risks with the equipment or with the topics they are covering.

ICT lessons can be stressful. It is hard to keep track of what everyone is doing and many classes resemble plate-spinning exercises as the teacher 'fire fights' and 'troubleshoots' all over the place. Little wonder that they find it hard to address the individual needs of pupils – they are too busy attending to the needs of the equipment.

This means that if we are not careful, the ICT classroom can be a very restrictive environment for some of the pupils. However, it is important to avoid making assumptions about pupils' technology skills.

Managing the inclusive classroom

It is hard to accept that many of the children you teach will have exceptionally good skills for certain aspects of computing. Just remember that one aspect of the inclusive classroom is sharing information, and a good teacher is one who doesn't mind being patronised by the 'experts' occasionally. You cannot know everything about every aspect of ICT – even Bill Gates can't do that and he's devoted years

> ## Michael Y10 EBD
>
> Michael, aged 15, has learning difficulties and behavioural problems. He has very limited literacy and his maths is restricted to adding up and taking away. He receives considerable assistance from the learning support base within a mainstream school. His TA, Sean, made many assumptions about Michael's ability to access a computer. He prepared simple worksheets with lots of pictures to go at the side of the machine and told Michael that they would work on the computer together. Michael thought this was very funny as his favourite pastime is downloading MP3 files and burning them onto a CD. He has offered to show Sean how to do this.

to it. You are there to manage the learning. It's up to you to set routines and expectations especially in the following areas:

- gaining pupils' attention at the start of the class

- deciding where pupils sit

- planning groupings for different activities

- deciding how often children with special needs are left to work on their own or with others, without a TA

- stopping pupils fiddling with their computers when you are trying to give whole-class instructions

- managing the end of the lesson when some people have finished practical work and others are still trying to print

- providing a variety of activities at different levels for different pupils

- providing extra work for quick finishers

Learning styles

ICT should be a subject which communicates on different levels to the majority of pupils. After all, it is very visual and has a strong element of cause and effect. Remember that people learn in different ways and there are many different routes to the same goal. We know that, for some children, movement stimulates the brain, yet pupils are constantly told to stop wandering about the room and get back to their seats. ICT lets pupils learn by looking, listening and doing, so it would appear counter-productive for teachers to stand at the front and talk.

Visual – learning by seeing

Pictures help for all sorts of reasons. They can overcome barriers for poor readers and provide additional support for pupils who are not confident language users.

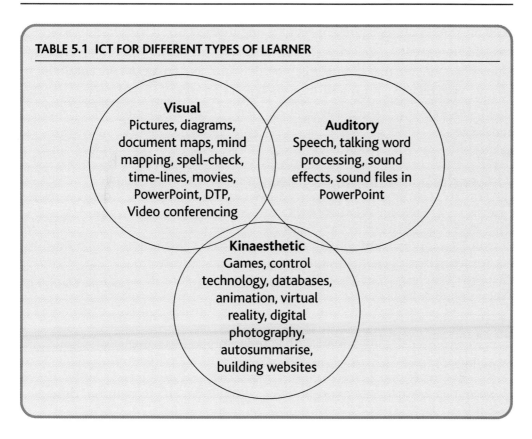

TABLE 5.1 ICT FOR DIFFERENT TYPES OF LEARNER

Many people just prefer pictures and would rather navigate from a map than from a set of written directions.

ICT can stimulate visual learning with graphics, animations and simulations. Interactive whiteboards and PowerPoint presentations let teachers present concepts in a visual way. Digital cameras help pupils to capture real-life images and use them in PowerPoint and publishing packages to make meaningful and relevant materials which motivate them. Timelines, mind mapping, diagrams, photos, video and graphs all help to develop visual intelligence. Animations from CD-ROMs such as the Dorling Kindersley *The Way Things Work* can help to teach concepts and, just as importantly, bring some light-hearted humour into the classroom.

Auditory – learning by hearing

Auditory learners prefer to learn through sound and speech, and in some schools, learners get plenty of practice! Many PCs, and all Tablet PCs, can record speech and sound. These files can then be embedded into slides or documents.

- Get children to use some of the sound clips in Encarta to explain concepts.

- Get pupils to create a video with voice-over and compare it with written text to see which works best.

- Use built-in sound recording in Office 2003 to embed the spoken word into presentations or essays.

- Use a microphone to dictate text into documents.

Listening does not necessarily mean listening to a teacher. ICT can also encourage conversation-based collaboration, for example through video conferencing. Remember, though, that listening is intensive and needs a lot of concentration, so it is not suitable for all learners. It is estimated that most learners switch off after about ten minutes, so use this sparingly and break it up with lots of talking and doing.

Kinaesthetic – learning by doing

Kinaesthetic or tactile learners prefer active forms of learning such as writing, drawing and producing animations, or making models and doing practical experiments. They benefit from using devices that involve touch, like mice and joysticks, or a Tablet PC, which enables users to write or draw onto a computer using a pen.

- Create computer games. Start with simple storyboards using PowerPoint; build game websites using FrontPage.

- Encourage learners to explore and play with design and formatting features.

eviations into AutoCorrect on the Tools menu.

- Give them hints and tips on using the facilities in PowerPoint and Word and then stand back aond let them at it.

Using suitable resources

Many teachers think in terms of print-based resources although this is now changing as they gather materials for the interactive whiteboard. One example might be to make a video to explain how to use a digital video camera to those who have not used one before. The video could be divided into a series of clips so that they can be downloaded more quickly. You can put them together again, either on a school network or burn them to CD so they can be used when required. You can also create PowerPoints to show different procedures. These can be made into handouts to use as a memory prompt.

Jenny Y7

Jenny in year 7 is enthusiastic to use the computer but does not always do things in the right order. Her teacher showed her how to save her work to a folder in *My Documents*. With help from a TA, Jenny made a crib sheet with very few words on it to remind her of what to do. Her mother later told the school that Jenny had successfully taught her grandparents how to save their work.

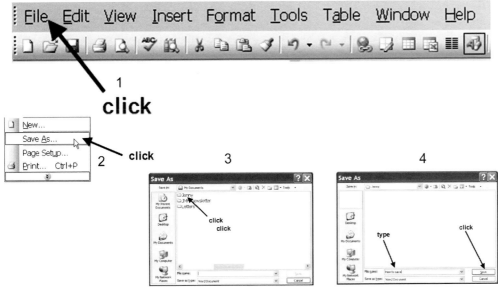

'How to save' – Jenny's crib sheet

Matching tasks to student abilities, aptitudes and interests

Students work in a variety of ways and bring different abilities and aptitudes to that work. Some are good at making materials look nice, others are good at manipulating images and have endless patience cropping and resizing pictures. Still others enjoy working with PowerPoint or getting involved in developing sophisticated style sheets for newsletters.

A school in Dudley encouraged pupils to come to after-school club to use the computers. Some pupils just wanted to play games or find music files on the Internet, but a surprising number of pupils were willing to work on teachers' handouts, typing them up and making them look good. This not only improved the pupils' word-processing skills but also increased the bank of materials held electronically. Less predictably, in some cases, the relationship between teacher and pupil improved as, for once, they were not so obviously on opposing sides.

Put the CD in the tray

Press the button to
close the tray

An example of a visual information sheet

Linking work to other areas of the curriculum

Chapter 8 looks more closely at the role of the ICT co-ordinator across the school. Needless to say, you will be quite popular with colleagues if you can find a way of linking their subject to the ICT curriculum. Also pupils will benefit because they come to see ICT as a skill for life that has relevance outside the classroom, and not just as a subject they do on alternate Monday afternoons. Many subjects lend themselves to database work:

● In French, people could be described under different categories, e.g. cheveux/yeux/âge/taille, etc.

● Pupils studying the Poor Law in history could use local history sources to find out about punishments in the workhouse, or look at the census for a particular district in their town in the mid-nineteenth century.

● Holidays and tourism would be a good choice for questionnaires.

● Modelling might be explored through the topic of healthy eating.

● An event might spark off a whole ICT project, as in the Play Bill project.

Example

Year 10 were producing *Macbeth* and were planning to do a dress rehearsal in front of the whole school and then three performances for parents and governors. This is what they did using ICT:

USING ICT TO SUPPORT A SCHOOL PRODUCTION

Programme	Word/clip art/digital photographs
Publicity trailer shown on parents' evening	Digital video of rehearsals, PowerPoint
Tickets	MS Publisher or Word/digital photographs
Hire of costumes/props	Internet
Lighting?	Draw program to plan set-up. Pre-programmed lighting sequences
Music	Cubase-devised music and sound effects
Modelling costings	Spreadsheet

Costing Macbeth

Below is a cost list for the school production of *Macbeth*. Obviously there are many variables when pricing a project of this nature: prices differ depending on the retailer, and the school may already have (or be able to make) certain items which can then be deducted from this list, such as costumes, PA, stage blocks, etc.

The list is as follows:

1 A portable lighting rig will need to be hired, assuming that the school doesn't already have one. Although it is possible to run a production without electric light, the atmosphere adopted in *Macbeth* lends itself to dark and moody scenes. The estimated cost of this is £300.

2 The school may also want to hire removable stacker-seats. Estimated cost £200.

3 Material for costumes. Pupils could make most costumes a relatively low cost.

4 Props such as a cauldron and stage weaponry. This depends on the school history of theatrical productions; certain items can be re-used from old productions, other items be made. Estimated cost £50–£100.

5 Marketing could consist of posters and letters which are then sent out to parents/guardians at no extra cost.

6 It is common practice for such evenings to provide free refreshments for the audience during the interval. Estimated cost £50–£70.

7 Music could be provided by the music students within the school. This would enable more students to become involved and would also save on money.

With a ticket price of £3 for an adult and £2 for a child the school would make all of this money back and might even turn a small profit. Please refer to the CD for a full working example.

COSTING A SCHOOL PRODUCTION

School production of Macbeth

OUTGOINGS	
hire lighting rig	£300.00
stacker seats	£200.00
material for capes and cloaks, nightgowns	£37.50
blood packets	£6.00
bowls of fruit	£4.00
bush	£5.99
candle	£0.80
cauldron with cups	£5.00
chalice with wine	£4.35
crown and sceptre	£5.95
dagger on belt	£6.00
daggers 8	£8.00
goblets 6	£6.00
key	£2.50
pikes and flags	£14.00
plastic turkey legs x6	£6.50
swords 6	£8.00
table	£0.00
throne	£8.00
thumb	£1.99
wineskin	£4.99
witches' masks 3	£18.00
TOTAL	**£653.57**

How many people will come each night?

Remember the school hall can only seat 200 people

Number of adults each night `107`
Number of children each night `59`

How many performances will we have?

Choose one, two or three nights `2`

How much income will we get?

		INCOME
Tickets sales		
Adults	`£3.00`	£642.00
Children	`£2.00`	£236.00
TOTAL INCOME		**£878.00**

Supporting Pupils

We know that some students need more help than others to complete a given task. If we provide help we are also providing differentiation by support.

At its simplest, differentiation by support may come down to the discussions that you have with your students. Whilst support for individual students is a vital ingredient in differentiated teaching, do bear in mind that:

- You can't teach each pupil separately.

- Some pupils don't like one-to-one conversations with the teacher.

- Pupils taught separately are not being included in the group.

Compared to many subjects, ICT lends itself to individual and small-group work. Often the teacher will be wandering around the room offering assistance to individuals. It is also relatively easy to see who can't remember/understand/concentrate when everyone else starts switching on their machines and getting going. This gives the teacher the chance to focus on those individuals personally, or direct the TA's attention towards them.

Features of a good ICT lesson

What makes a good lesson? There is no magic formula and not even a set routine which works. Nevertheless there are some common features which tend to occur in the best lessons (see page 80).

- *Before* – careful planning to cover content; set objectives; plan for additional, supplementary or alternative activities for individual pupils; resources gathered and set up on machines/ intranet/ whiteboards/ back-ups on OHT in case of technology failure.

- *Opening of lesson* – Whole-class activities; plenary discussion; questioning; setting the pace; groups organised at start without too much intervention by pupils; busy purposeful atmosphere; questioning and discussion; attempt to engage interest and make introduction to activities relevant to pupils.

- *Development of lesson* – mix of computer and non-computer activities as appropriate; reinforcing the objectives again; a choice and range of purposeful and relevant activities; teacher intervention aware of particular needs, e.g. Harry needs to have different screen colour combinations for easy reading; Steven needs to be kept on task and have at least three different things to attempt; Jenny and Susan will not take notes; Matt will drift off if left to his own devices.

- *End* – making sure everyone has seen the whole as well as the parts; chance for pupils to see other people's work; pupils with clear understanding of what the objectives were and what they have done as individuals; pupils clear about what they need to do for homework and what will happen next week; ensuring that anyone who needs to have written notes has them.

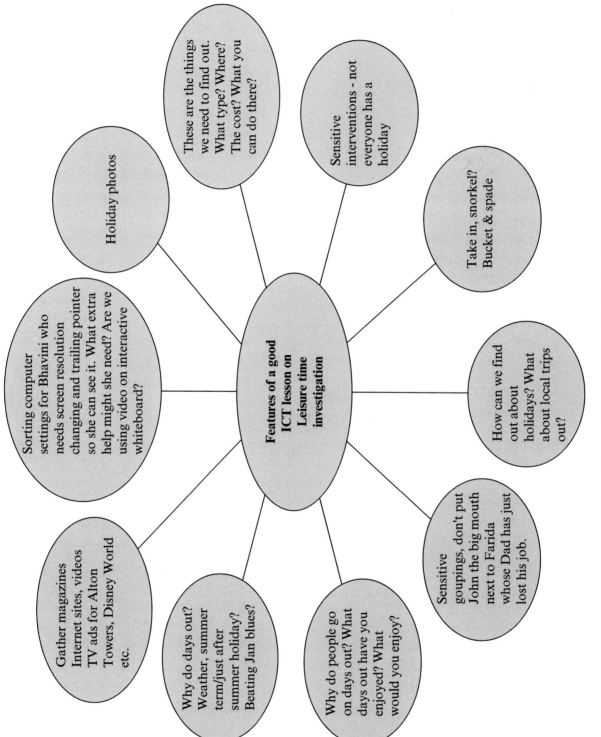

Features of a good ICT lesson on leisure time investigation

Monitoring and Assessment

Message boards and chatrooms are a great place to find out what pupils really think of subjects and teachers. Here are some extracts from a discussion on a BBC site about choosing options in Year 9. The original query was this:

> im going into yr.9 next yr so i will have to take options towards the end, as i sed im gud but i dont no how an I.T. gcse will be taken sum1 plz tell me

Opinions were divided as you will see from these answers:

> I'm gonna do ICT GNVQ, anyways I took it because alot of jobs are to do with computers even stuff like shop assistant so I'm taking it to make my job options wider. I've not started it yet so I can't say what its actually like but I've been told its writing as well as on the PC

> no dont take it. its quite easy but its borin n da corsework iz a load of rubbish.
> if i wld ave known wot it woz gonna b like i wldnt have taken it. i rele dnt lke it.

> IM GOING IN YEAR 10 NOW AND I TOOK I.T MY ADVISE TO YOU IS IF I.T CONCERNS THE JOB YOU WANT TO DO TAKE IT. IN SOME SCHOOL YOU CAN GET HALF A GSCE

> I've just finished yr10 and I've enjoyed GCSE ICT a lot. 60% of GCSE ICT is coursework so as you can imagine you spend most of the time doing your coursework. The Coursework is actually quite fun, especially the first project about communications because I incorporated it into my webdesign skills and made a site. The theory is a bit of a drag but not all that hard to understand. And to think my mum nearly talked me into taking History instead!!! I'm glad I took ICT . . .

> There is a lot of coursework, and yeah it probably is one of the longer GCSE's you could take, but it is worth it. Nowadays all companys for jobs are looking for ICT skilled people

> Hi there, I am now going into 5 year and I picked GCSE I.C.T and I love it. It is easy and so is the coursework. This is what I think but at the end of the day its up to you

What emerges quite strongly is that pupils see ICT as an essential subject when it comes to getting a job, 'even stuff like shop assistant' but they have problems with the volume and relevance of course work. 'It's writing as well as on the PC' says one pupil, which suggests that many pupils would prefer a more hands-on course. Comments such as, 'The theory is a bit of a drag' show that pupils would rather do practical activities than learn about the Data Protection Act or different ways of recording and recalling data.

The QCA view is:

> Information and communication technology (ICT) capability is an essential skill for life and enables learners to participate in a rapidly changing world . . . The national curriculum for ICT is designed to equip young people with the ability to use technological tools to find, explore, analyse, exchange, and present information responsibly and with discrimination. They learn how to employ ICT to enable rapid access to ideas and experiences from a wide range of people, communities and cultures.[1]

This is a far cry from the pupil's response: 'Its borin n da corsework iz a load of rubbish.' This chapter looks at how and why we should assess and what can be done to make ICT more applicable to students with special educational needs.

Why assess?

Assessment is vital for all sorts of reasons. Not only does it show how well the class is doing, but it also shows up the strengths and weaknesses of your own teaching. As this example from a teacher in Devon shows:

> I thought I had taught data capture forms really well but most of the class missed the deadline for having the course work submitted and when I saw the few that had come in, I realised why. They hadn't got a clue. They had missed the point, or rather the point was not clear enough for them to know what they were doing.
>
> There are lots of pupils who don't organise project work well. They have lots of scraps of paper with no dates or page numbers on, and often the work is illegible. This experience made me evaluate how I had explained the topic.
>
> In addition, with project work which can take up to half a term to complete, it's hard to keep an eye on who can't do it. In the old days, when it was separate bits of homework each week or short tests in class, you could see where the problem lay and do something about it. Now if you don't pick it up from body language or questioning the right pupils at the right moment, it is easy to miss the quiet child who doesn't know what to do.

Teachers need to stand back occasionally and see how they are dealing with the varying needs of pupils. Look particularly at pupils who have mobility problems or who are not attending regularly. Ask yourself whether there is any difference between girls' and boys' work. Individual pieces of work will provide partial evidence of each key stage level, but pupils will need to keep a 'portfolio' of coursework.

Pupil-friendly language

Obviously it helps to have a glossary of the terms used in ICT lessons (see Appendix 6.2) but make sure that the language used in the exempla materials is straightforward too (see Appendix 6.1). Many pupils can understand the technology but not the carrier language – the language used by the teacher to set a task or test – so they find it hard to show what they can do. Pupils with a hearing impairment and many with language disorders may interpret words literally so that 'discuss' becomes 'talk to your friends about' rather than 'think and write about'. Also, beware of using analogies. All too often a teacher gives a graphic example to illustrate a concept or general point, only to find that a pupil has homed in on this and cannot see the wider picture. Think about the way you phrase questions for all formal and informal tasks, tests and resource materials.[2]

A very popular way of conveying objectives to pupils is WALTS, WILFS and TIBS:

WALTS	We are learning to . . .
WILF	What I am looking for . . .
TIBS	This is because . . .

Unit 7.1

Lesson 1

We are learning to organise the content for a presentation
What I am looking for is the ability to consider the needs of the audience
This is because content and organisation are the most important parts of an effective presentation[3]

Ways of assessing achievement

Some assessment will come from teacher observation and conversation with pupils. Talking to pupils is a particularly good way of assessing whether the work they do at school stretches them to the limits of their potential or whether they are capable of more advanced work, perhaps because of skills and understanding acquired at home. The checklist on page 84 may help you to record progress.

Too often we make assumptions about pupils, especially those with special educational needs. You need to see the whole person and not the disability as the following example shows:

We assumed large single press switches would be necessary for David to take photographs. We were wrong: David turned down the proffered switch and asked to have a go with the ordinary button on the camera. By setting the camera on a tripod at an accessible height and with adult verbal support, David pressed the button with his forefinger.[4]

CHECKLIST FOR RECORDING PUPIL PROGRESS

	Yes	No	??
Can they remember work previously done?			
Can they remember sequences?			
Do they understand what they are doing?			
Can they apply old knowledge to new situations?			
Can they navigate confidently around desktop and folders?			
Can they save and retrieve work?			
Can they insert graphics and clip art?			
Can they make own decisions about when to use ICT?			
Do they use ICT out of school?			
Can they use the computer independently?			
Are they aware of the role of ICT in the wider world?			

Some schools use self-assessment sheets like the one that follows.

SELF-ASSESSMENT SHEETS

Name ....
Class ....
Date ....
Graphics

Level One
I can make marks using the mouse.

Level Two
I can open and change colours.
I can change brush size, colour and texture.
I can change painting/drawing tools.
I can rub out mistakes.
I can print work.
I can save work.

Level Three
I can insert clip art into a piece of written work.
I can scan pictures into the computer.
I can use a digital camera and import pictures into the computer.

Level Four
I can use an object-based graphics package to produce images and visual models.

But, of course, pupils may tell 'fibs' and are rarely impartial in their assessment of their own abilities. So it makes sense to have mini assessments where you check the skills in a short piece of work before launching them on more extensive course work. In that case, a tick list which the teacher checks against the work may help:

GRAPHICS AND CLIP ART

Task	Completed (date)
Geometrical shapes	
Fill	
Line styles	
Add text to graphics	
Modify graphics	
Group objects	
Export objects	

There is a range of external examinations, but most pupils do one of the following: CLAIT, Short course GCSE, Full GCSE and GNVQ. However, some pupils need to have recognition for smaller steps of achievement.

P levels

A good starting point is *the Key Stage 3 Materials for Teaching ICT Capability at and below level 3*.[5] These materials provide case studies and resources to help teachers provide for pupils working within the range P1 to P3, P4–P8 and levels 1–3.

They aim to support the three principles of the inclusion statement:

- setting suitable learning challenges

- responding to pupils' diverse learning needs

- overcoming potential barriers to learning and assessment

They will enable schools to select alternative activities and resources to support objectives, and 'offer activities that are engaging, have age-related contexts and are stimulating and exciting.'[6] So far, the schools which have trialled them seem pleased.

> All of our pupils have been able to succeed at some level.
> This has increased our expectations of what our pupils can achieve and heightened our awareness of ICT capability as a whole staff.[7]

> The case study and resources for 7.4 enabled our pupils to understand rules and variables within a model. Our pupils have severe or multiple learning difficulties, sensory impairments and some in addition have autism. Until now our assumption had been that modelling was beyond their capabilities. The materials challenged our misconceptions and through appropriate, interactive resources our pupils were able to engage and learn. What a success![8]

This publication also provides a handy reference to the key vocabulary needed throughout Key Stage 3 and, indeed, for much of Key Stage 4 work. This is reproduced in Appendix 6.2 and is on the CD-ROM as you may wish to use it in onscreen grids or handouts.

Another excellent resource to use in conjunction with the P scales is the 'Information and Communication Technology Syllabus' written by Sophie Garner at Sunfield School and distributed through SENIT Forum (Special Educational Needs Information Technology). This covers 'Communicating Information', 'Handling Information', 'Modelling', 'Measurement and Control', and 'Application and Effects' in great detail.[9]

Entry Level Certificate

This certificate is aimed at candidates working at levels 1, 2 and 3 of the National Curriculum or at candidates seeking a first qualification in basic ICT. It is offered by several examination boards and is assessed by means of four units of course work each focusing on a different use of IT. The course can be undertaken by students of any age and could contribute to a GCSE in future years.

Special arrangements for external exams

Once you have decided on an appropriate qualification, think about whether special arrangements will be necessary for individual pupils. Examination boards are bound by SENDA and will be covered by Part III of the Act. This means that candidates cannot be treated less favourably on the grounds of their disability in an exam setting. Exam boards are generally quite helpful about the special requirements for particular pupils to show their achievements. The Joint Council for General Qualifications issues guidance to exam boards and to centres, as shown opposite:

The future of assessment

In the future, computer systems will change the way we think about examinations. Already in place are computerised administration systems which speed up the paperwork and keep costs down and electronic portfolios for GCSE course work. It is early days yet but QCA are trialling a test to provide an independent measure of pupils' attainment in information and communication technology (ICT) at Key Stage 3. The test will be on-screen and will assess pupils' ICT capability across levels 3 to 8 of the National Curriculum. The test will be marked automatically and verified by human markers. At OCR, they already have electronic assessment of practical tasks in CLAIT and on-screen tests for Key Skills and Basic Skills. Centres like these tests because they get an instant result. What is delaying e-assessment is the provision of ICT in schools. According to OCR, centres with a high number of entries often prefer to use the paper-based examination option because the number of candidates is too great to allow access to a sufficient number of PCs. OCR are monitoring candidate performance in paper-based versus electronic formats carefully, but so far there is no evidence of discrepancy.

Summary of principles for centres

The centre should:

7.1 choose the qualification or the option(s) within a qualification which is most appropriate for the candidate with a known long-term or permanent disability or learning difficulty. The requirements of the candidate and the implications for the assessment should be considered when he/she applies for a course;

7.2 recognise the requirements of each candidate individually making use of specialist advice from external sources, as appropriate;

7.3 ensure that all applications for special arrangements and special consideration are supported by the Head of Centre and are submitted no later than the due dates;

7.4 ensure that the arrangements requested will assist the candidate to demonstrate his/her attainment without affecting or circumventing assessment requirements;

7.5 consider the candidate's normal way of learning and producing work as a basis for special arrangements provided that this would not give the candidate an unfair advantage or compromise the integrity of the examination or assessment;

7.6 ensure that the candidate has experience of and practice in the use of the arrangements requested.

Schools need to ensure that special assessment arrangements do not give unfair advantage over other candidates.

The arrangements may include extra time, additional facilities or some level of support. For example, pupils with a physical disability may be allowed a writer, extra time allowance (normally 25%) and mechanical/electronic aids. Students with a visual impairment may have a writer, a reader, tapes, question papers with large print, Braille or Moon, use of a keyboard to produce typescript answers or raised type responses to a question paper, extra time allowance (normally 25%) and mechanical/electronic equipment. Awarding bodies will not provide enlarged question papers for candidates with such difficulties, but centres may, with the permission of the awarding body, open question papers up to one hour prior to the examination in order to make enlargements or photocopy onto coloured paper. Centres must take responsibility for ensuring that the entire paper is copied and for maintaining the security of the question paper.

Arrangements for pupils with a hearing impairment may include the use of a communicator/interpreter, extra time allowance (normally 25%) and mechanical/electronic aids. Signing of questions or the oral presentation of questions using the oral/aural approach may be permitted for candidates with a hearing impairment (except where reading is an assessment objective) in exceptional circumstances, if either approach is the usual method of communication in the classroom and access to the examination cannot be achieved by other means. Special amplification for aural tests may be permitted for hearing-impaired candidates. Reading of the tests to enable candidates to lip-read may also be permitted. In addition, candidates whose hearing loss results in a linguistic disability may be provided with question papers with appropriate modified wording, as recommended by a specialist teacher of the deaf.

In the case of candidates with specific learning difficulties of a dyslexic or similar nature, arrangements may include a writer and/or a reader, extra time allowance (normally 25%), tapes and typescripts of answers and coloured overlays/paper. Some visual difficulties are normally corrected by the use of tinted spectacles or coloured overlays, and permission for the use of these aids does not have to be sought from the awarding body. Arrangements for candidates with other learning difficulties may include a writer and/or a reader, extra time allowance (normally 25%) and other audio/visual aids as appropriate to the needs of the individual.

References

1   QCA 'About information and communication technology': http://www.qca.org.uk/7889.html

2   For carrier language see: http://www.standards.dfes.gov.uk/primary/features/inclusion/942579/

3   From 'ICT pages for Derby City': http://ngfl.derby.gov.uk/sii/Support/ks3/ict.htm

4   Singleton, E., Ross, I. and Flavell, E. (2003) *Access to ICT*. London: David Fulton Publishers.

5   DfES (2004) Key Stage 3 *Materials for teaching ICT capability at and below level 3 – Guide for senior leaders and subject leaders*. London: HMSO 0382-2004.

6   Ibid p. 7

7   Ibid p. 5

8   Ibid p. 7

9   'Information and Communication Technology Syllabus', SENIT Forum: http://atschool.eduweb.co.uk/meldreth/textandinfo/ICT.html

10 Ofsted Update for Inspectors No 36 – August 2001 *Inspecting information and communications technology (ICT)*.

Managing Support

In 2003 the Government stated its intention, through the Standards Fund to provide £268 million specifically for support staff salaries and £37.45 million for their training during 2003–04.[1] Good support staff make teaching a very pleasant and enjoyable job. Getting the wrong staff can make it a nightmare. In the ICT classroom you are likely to have two different types of support: the TA (Teaching Assistant) whose job it is to support the pupils, and the ICT technician whose job it is to maintain, and possibly troubleshoot, problems with the equipment. Their roles and responsibilities are very different in most schools.

What does a TA do?

A TA may have a myriad of jobs but these broadly divide into three types of work:

- working with one pupil
- providing additional support for a larger group
- developing and maintaining resources and records

Providing support for individual pupils

- being an advocate or go-between
- understanding how the child learns
- identifying barriers to learning
- keeping the child on task
- knowing the child's strengths, weaknesses and flashpoints
- building confidence
- increasing the pupil's independence
- devising strategies to increase the pupil's concentration span

- helping the pupil keep track of homework and course work

- helping the pupil to organise themselves – essential equipment, school bag, time management

- considering alternative ways in which the pupil could work

The TA may act as an observer. Where a particular child is causing concern, then you may want to find out how much time is being spent on learning. This is a particularly effective exercise when used with the child who never misbehaves but is listless and not making the progress expected. While the teacher is presenting to the whole class or going around working with individual children on machines, the TA can keep an eye on individuals. This works well in ICT because pupils are often looking at monitors and may not be so aware of an adult's scrutiny. It may help to add in times to see if the child starts well and goes 'off the boil' or takes time to adjust to the pace of the lesson.

TA OBSERVATION OF A PUPIL

Time	Activity	On task?
10.45	Listening to instructions	No
10.50	Opening spreadsheet	No (talking to Frederica)
10.52	Inserting data	Yes but slow
11.15	Working in pairs	Yes – with Aphar – quite competitive!

This sort of activity may help to answer the elusive question 'What works?'

Danger Point! Whose job is it, anyway?

Sometimes a TA can be almost too good, as in this example:
'Natalie is fantastic. She is full of energy and is a real powerhouse. The deputy head thinks the world of her and is only too grateful to offload work. There is an attitude of 'Let's leave it to Natalie.' Some of the staff let her make decisions about pupils which are well beyond the remit of a TA's role. It is very divisive. The other TAs feel resentful that they are not treated in the same way and inexperienced staff feel a little threatened and overwhelmed by this totally confident young woman who seems to be running the place.'

Roles must be clearly defined. Natalie can offer advice about differentiation to teachers but it should be clear that the teacher has responsibility.

Working on alternative approaches to learning which may benefit all children

Alternative approaches to learning may include:

- helping to break down new materials into manageable chunks

- changing the format of materials

- producing additional materials which cover gaps in prior knowledge

- developing alternative ways of presenting information, e.g. tapes/diagrams

- developing alternative ways of recording achievement, e.g. digital pictures

- creating talking worksheets/ICT word banks/writing frames to help pupils compose text

- producing support materials

- developing good learning strategies for all pupils, e.g. mindmaps

It is a useful exercise to audit the pupils' abilities at the beginning of each school year and this is where the TA is invaluable. Some children are not good at using the mouse or keyboard but this can be overlooked as the teacher concentrates on classroom management, behaviour, the curriculum or assessment. Sometimes the child has poor motor control or has sat back and let the other half of their pair do the inputting. It might be a gender issue or passivity. It can also be a fear of looking a fool, especially if others in the class have good ICT facilities at home.

Danger Point! You need to communicate

Rob, a TA, was irate when he had spent an afternoon simplifying and enlarging materials for a class using Publisher, only to find that the teacher had changed her mind and they were looking at databases instead. She had forgotten to tell him. Not only had Rob wasted his time but Bhavini could not make head nor tail of the lesson. 'Adapting materials is not a goodwill gesture,' said Rob, 'it is the difference between Bhavini being able to be part of the class or being totally excluded.'

Assisting with classroom resources and records

Some support staff like to have a clear and separate role, while others prefer to be involved in classes and with individual pupils.

Danger Point! Have a clear job description

Val had trained to get a specialist qualification in dyslexia and was keen to use her expertise to support children in the lower school. She was horrified when she discovered that the school expected her to spend her time photocopying, inputting data and collecting money.

'When I talked about supporting pupils, I thought it meant class contact. I don't want clerical work and if I did, office work is better paid!' she said.

There are plenty of opportunities for TAs to be involved at several levels. Equipment will always be an issue – the printer that jams, the monitor that flickers, dead machines, mice which stick. The TA may be able to correct some of these and should be encouraged to do so. Another solution is to have a 'Problems Book' in the ICT suite and get the TA to jot down notes about any items which are not working satisfactorily and to follow them up. Sometimes the TA will be responsible for the maintenance of individual pupils' laptops, charging batteries, etc.

According to the DfES, there are 24 non-teaching tasks which teachers routinely perform. It is envisaged that in the future some of these will be delegated to TAs and admin. staff:

1 Collecting money

2 Chasing absences

3 Bulk photocopying

4 Copy typing

5 Producing standard letters

6 Producing class lists

7 Record-keeping and filing

8 Classroom display

9 Analysing attendance figures

10 Processing exam results

11 Collating pupil reports

12 Administering work experience

13 Administering examinations

14 Administering teacher cover

15 ICT troubleshooting and minor repairs

16 Commissioning new ICT equipment

17 Ordering supplies and equipment

18 Stocktaking

19 Cataloguing, preparing, issuing and maintaining equipment and materials

20 Minuting meetings

21 Co-ordinating and submitting bids

22 Seeking and giving personnel advice

23 Managing pupil data

24 Inputting pupil data.[2]

Christopher Y8 Problems with mobility, balance and visual perception

Christopher is a Year 8 pupil in Haywards Heath and has problems with mobility, balance and visual perception. The school is addressing some of the issues which crop up if pupils are supplied with expensive and heavy ICT equipment.

Pam, the SENCO at the school said, 'A laptop is quite a lot for a child to carry about all day, particularly with their other belongings. We gave his TA the responsibility for its transport around the building and during school-time. As we are charged with its safety, provision also had to be made for its secure storage at break and lunchtime'. (AbilityNet case study).

What do computer support staff do?

A quick look at the job descriptions posted on the Becta site 'Job descriptions for ICT technical support staff' http://www.becta.org.uk/techcomp/jobs.cfm shows a range of tasks.

As you might expect, the job varies vastly from school to school. Some schools want an emphasis on technical skills where the technician is responsible for password protection and network security; in other schools, technicians supervise pupils and have a teaching/demonstration role. Here are some of the most common duties:

Technical

- undertake routine maintenance with the network manager
- update the network with software as and when required
- in the absence of the network manager, ensure that the network is backed up each day
- keep hardware/software/network in good working order
- ensure physical security of work stations and monitors
- ensure all printers are loaded with paper and ink
- set up IT equipment as and when required by IT staff and non-specialist staff

Administrative

- produce operating instructions for equipment and software
- change staff and pupil passwords as required
- create new users as required
- maintain an inventory of all software and hardware
- send equipment for repair
- provide network manager with up-to-date information on departmental spending each month
- photocopy and collate resources for the department
- draw up and submit orders in liaison with the network manager
- assist in maintaining a database of all ICT equipment
- working with the pupil, teacher and others, collect information relating to computer access needs. Liaising with the ICT technician, create individual access profiles

Teaching and supervision

- supervise rooms at lunchtime and after school
- supervise the library in absence of librarian as required
- assist pupils using software – generic office

- demonstrate software to pupils and staff

- assist staff with ICT queries in the classroom

- support staff using ICT to teach pupils as required

- share examples of good practice

- train technical assistants

- assist in the production of worksheets and course notes

Of course, the best support goes beyond looking at equipment and staff needs, as this example from AbilityNet shows:

Rory Y7 Congenital Nystagmus

Rory, a Year 7 pupil, has congenital Nystagmus – a visual impairment making reading and writing very difficult. Rory had used an Alphasmart 3000 to record his work in primary school, but, with no way of enlarging the font size, he was struggling to read text back. A laptop was an ideal solution, with modifications to the operating system to improve visual access, including a change of colour scheme, the size of the icons, the accessibility settings in Internet Explorer and the shape and dimensions of the mouse pointer.

In-school technician support is an essential factor in Rory's success. From the outset, he was assigned a ICT 'buddy' to sort out any technical problems he encounters. His buddy also set up training sessions for both Rory and his mother on the use and application of the laptop – to promote home-school continuity and enable Rory's parents to take an active role in his education. In addition, Rory was issued with his own photocopier pass enabling him to make his own decisions about the support he requires and enlarge any worksheets or other classroom materials independently as and when he needs them.

(AbilityNet case study)

Guidelines for new TAs

Some TAs have had training or are naturally suited to the work but others will need support. Every teacher they work with will probably have different rules or styles of teaching. Some teachers like the computer room to be a quiet, calm environment, while others encourage lots of discussion and group work, and welcome participation at all levels. General rules might include:

- Look at the pupils when you speak – not at the monitor. Some pupils will need to focus on you if they are to listen. Others might need to lip read.

- If you notice any problems or misunderstandings, clarify them immediately.

- Catch pupils being good – especially the difficult ones.

- Praise a good attempt.

- Never embarrass a student who gets it wrong – even if you know they are not trying.

- Never do the work for a pupil.

- Collaboration is not the same as copying. Try to stop plagiarism.

Hands Off!

- Never take over a keyboard

- Explain

- Demonstrate

- Delete or undo

- Instruct while pupil does it

- Teacher or TA writes it down or draws it for future reference

- Pupil repeats skill until it is fixed

Barriers to success

Sometimes the teacher and TA do not develop a smooth working relationship. Sometimes there is a personality clash; sometimes a conflict of expectations.

Megan Y10 wheelchair user

Megan, a Year 10 wheelchair user, is very outgoing, loud and tough. She has upset a number of the less experienced Classroom Assistants, including Margot, who is quite an anxious, motherly sort of person. Things came to a head in the ICT lesson because Megan wanted to sit with her friends and get one of them to do her text inputting and Margot wanted her to work on her own, which would have meant her working in a corner. Last week Megan lost her temper and swore at Margot, who left the room in tears.

   Trevor, the ICT teacher feels aggrieved: 'It's like having two kids in the classroom. Margot is supposed to be supporting Megan and, indirectly, supporting me. So how come I spent my break counselling her? Megan is out of order but is it my job or Margot's to sort her out? The demarcation lines are blurred and I'm getting it in the neck from both sides!'

(For guidance on working with TAs, see Appendix 7.)

Fear of technology

It is sometimes erroneously assumed that young people, fresh from college, know all about computers. After all, they grew up with them. They have been word processing essays since GCSE days and use email and Internet for their own purposes. Older people will be less confident and will need more hand holding. That is conventional wisdom, but it is certainly not borne out by experience. A lot comes down to individuals, their personality, life experience, and possibly their financial status too.

Many young people may have relied on using a friend's computer and have relatively few skills. Older people may have their own computer and regularly email grandchildren across the world. Make no assumptions. What is unforgivable is not to establish how much the TA knows and give them the chance to update and extend their skills. Some schools make a point of lending a laptop to the TA for the holidays. 'It's the least we can do,' said one teacher, 'as we don't pay them when they are not in school.'

It is important that new TAs are shown how to use the school ICT system. Even confident ICT users can be confused when confronted by a new network. If they don't sort this out initially, they may be embarrassed to ask basic questions later and waste time muddling their way through. A simple illustrated guide to the school system, clearly outlining procedures such as logging on, saving work, finding work, printing and accessing permissions to the system will enable the TA to work confidently with pupils.

Encourage TAs to watch demonstrations and the introductions to new topics. They may initially only be one step ahead of the pupils, but if they are frequent visitors to the ICT area, they will soon develop a good working knowledge. Ideally, information about forthcoming topics should be given to TAs supporting pupils with special needs. This will also help to build personal confidence and give them the opportunity to try things out.

Pupil mentor

Olivia is a TA in a large secondary school in Lancashire, she reports, 'Since I've been working here, my IT skills have improved. I could word process a bit before I started but it was more like copy typing and I was really slow. In fact when I came to the school, I could write by hand faster than I could type.'

Fortunately, Tracey, the head of ICT, was keen that everyone should be as enthusiastic as she was about the technology. She found a Year 10 boy, Ryan, who was really good at ICT and got him to help me every Friday lunchtime. He loved it because he was in charge. He was really strict! Tracey made a list of things she wanted me to learn and we did one or two each week. Now I can change text to columns for a newsletter, use word art for posters, callouts on the drawing toolbar for labelling activities, insert clipart and textboxes, size digital photographs and know how to copy to disc.

One of the great things is that as your confidence grows, you start to think of things you can do. I am really interested in the digital camera and the effect it has on pupils. I often take pictures of the pupils and some of them who don't think much of themselves are quite pleased when they see a picture where they are smiling. They never say much but you can see them looking at the printout, thinking, 'Is that really me?'

Build on strengths. A TA working with an individual pupil will become an 'expert' on their ICT support needs. This is a good starting point to build confidence in those who have little experience with technology or a fear of all things connected with computing.

References

[1] DfES (February 2003) *Working with Teaching Assistants in Secondary Schools.* London: HMSO 0115/2003.
[2] From DfEE circular 2/98.

Supporting other Staff in School

The government paper *Fulfilling The Potential* gives a good starting point for understanding the basic tenets which underpin current thinking on ICT in education:

> 'Working through the Government's primary and secondary education strategies, and the workforce remodelling agenda, our aims for the next stage of development will therefore be to ensure that for all schools:

> ● ICT makes a significant contribution to teaching and learning across all subjects and ages, inside and outside the curriculum;

> ● ICT is used to improve access to learning for pupils with a diverse range of individual needs, including those with SEN and disabilities;

> ● ICT is used as a tool for whole-school improvement;

> ● ICT is used as a means of enabling learning to take place more easily beyond the bounds of the formal school organisation and outside the school day – and of enhancing the quality of such experiences; and

> ● ICT capabilities are developed as key skills essential for participation in today's society and economy.'[1]

Every school should have a whole-school ICT policy because ICT has an impact on the work of the whole school. Not only does it run across all curriculum areas but also it is the lifeblood of administration and management systems too. In many schools, the ICT co-coordinator is likely to be a jack of all trades and master of many. Whilst not necessarily responsible for all aspects of ICT, the co-ordinator will probably have a role in:

● developing an ICT policy for the school

● resource management

● maintenance agreements

- management information systems

- monitoring the Key Stage 3, Key Stage 4 ICT

- monitoring ICT usage across all National Curriculum subjects

- technical support

- staff training

And of course the co-ordinator needs to be a font of all knowledge, keeping up to date with relevant hardware and software developments.

The Ofsted progress report states:

'The co-ordination of ICT demands a considerable range of expertise, requiring good ICT understanding and knowledge, technical skills and the ability to provide professional support. Too many demands are placed on some ICT co-ordinators, most of whom have a full teaching commitment and few opportunities for monitoring the subject adequately across the school. In recognition of the demands of the role, larger primary, middle and secondary schools increasingly have more than one member of staff involved in the co-ordination of ICT . . .'[2]

There are a number of suggestions for dividing up the responsibilities:

- A senior manager, possibly a deputy head, undertakes strategic ICT co-ordination and resource deployment across the school, monitors how well ICT is embedded in administration functions and curriculum delivery, and also what impact the investment is having on standards.

- An ICT subject leader/Head of Department oversees core ICT courses and is involved in aspects of staff training.

- An ICT systems manager deals with network developments and management, and the intranet and website, and liaises with external providers of services and products.

- A bursar manages management information systems.

- An ICT technician provides day-to-day technical support.

- The staff of each department/faculty have responsibility for developing the use of ICT within their subject.

- A professional development manager's duties include co-ordinating the staff's ICT training needs.

With the complexity of whole-school ICT, it is useful to have a strategic ICT group, comprising core personnel, to propose and discuss priorities and developments. 'Moving from co-ordinator to co-ordination'[3] is a paper on the ICT advice site which looks at different models. One issue with this approach is that it might not lead to joined-up thinking. Everyone has their own area of expertise or their own little empire, and provision becomes patchy and fragmented. Some schools have a working party which decides priorities and ensures that developments cascade to the teaching staff.

Safety and other key policies

ICT can enhance pupils' learning experience in all subjects. It offers an enormous range and depth of information, access to original source materials, a variety of media and instantaneous communication via the Web and email. It will change the way we experience life and work. It is vital that young people have the chance to experience these new technologies which will be a key part of their everyday lives.

Nevertheless, like all knowledge, it carries risks. There is a good chance that young people will access unsuitable materials. They have, of course, always been able to find print material which others might deem unsuitable. The difference with the Web and email is that some of the material may come looking for them. They may be exposed to material, situations or communications that are undesirable or make them feel vulnerable.

Internet safety is everyone's responsibility. Make sure all the staff, including support staff, understand and implement the following policies and practices:

- provision of pupil information/photographs via a school website

- methods for providing Internet safety education for pupils

- provision of group or individual pupil email addresses in school

- measures to prevent bullying and harassment of pupils when online

- the use of instant messaging and chat rooms, whether for educational or social purposes

- anti-virus practices which should include policies on floppy disks and other removable media, downloading files and email attachments

(See Appendix 8 for an acceptable use policy which is also on the CD-ROM.)

The ICT vision

In all the welter of rules and restrictions, we sometimes overlook the fact that ICT is intended to make things better, to make lessons more exciting and increase the opportunities for children to have meaningful educational experiences. The classroom of the future will have considerably more technology and this will affect teaching and learning. The scenario found in the DfES vision document *Transforming the way we learn* is based on the 'day in the life' of a pupil. It may serve as a useful starting point for staff discussions.

A day in the life of . . .

. . . a pupil in a secondary school that is effectively integrating e-learning with traditional learning techniques.

Uzman arrives in school at 8.30 and goes straight to the open learning area. He logs on to retrieve some marked homework ready for today's English lesson. Last night he completed two homework assignments on his home computer and stored these in his user area on the school system. His friend Jenny had also done the same, but had borrowed one of the school's laptops as she has no computer at home. As they look at their marked homework they discuss what they did for last night's assignments . . .

. . . After assembly, the first period is GNVQ science, in which digital learning materials on the school's intranet feature prominently. Currently, pupils are working through these in a three-week block. Uzman works independently on the unit on physical forces and regularly discusses his experiences with other pupils doing this topic, through a virtual learning community of which he is a member. However, he knows that he can e-mail his science teacher to seek help with any assessment tasks he has not understood. He also knows that, for this lesson, the teacher has prioritised direct support for another group of pupils who are having rather more difficulty with some of the ideas than he is . . .

. . . Fourth period and it's off to the D&T workshop, where Uzman's group are currently working on a CADCAM project, using a sophisticated design package. Uzman gets into a discussion with the teacher and three other pupils about the design of the photograph frames they are working on. The teacher tries to get the group to develop their designs so that they are more adventurous and unusual. As a result of this, Uzman goes to one of the available machines and tries out various changes to his design. He stores these in his user area and decides to look at them later, working from home . . .

. . . Uzman is following a GCSE short course in ICT and this comes next. The class is currently working on the validity and bias of data. The lesson takes place in an ordinary classroom in which the teacher has access to a fixed computer on the network and the Internet. Using digital projection facilities, the teacher visits a site for an environmental lobby group and compares this with a Government site on global warming. A lively discussion ensues and the class works in small groups to identify what clues to look for in a website address and in the content available on entry to the site . . .

. . . The school operates a 'seventh period' session in which pupils can voluntarily follow the activity of their choice. This includes a range of clubs and other extra-curricular activities. Uzman goes to the 'ICT for all' club, where he is working with three other pupils on the development of parts of the school's website. They are creating pages about the school's sports teams and are including digital video clips that they have filmed and edited.[4]

Many staff will give a wry smile as they read the description above. Somehow, pupils in DfES case studies always seem a little keener and livelier than the ones we meet in the classroom. Presumably the classroom of the future will come with more biddable children!

Carrying the staff with you

Some staff will be very enthusiastic users of ICT. They will use it naturally and spontaneously and will be keen to embed it in their lessons and encourage children to use it as just another tool in the classroom, alongside books, discussion, pair work, role play, investigations, etc. Other staff will need to be encouraged. Let's look at different technologies and how they might be exploited by your colleagues. Word, PowerPoint and digital images are all powerful tools which can be used in every subject with good results. Word can be used in a creative way to combine images and text. Worksheets can be personalised with Word Art or different fonts, and colour combinations of text and paper to meet different pupils' needs. Templates for electronic worksheets, for newspapers and reports can be easily compiled and will look good.

Form fields

In science, a quiz could be created using the Forms toolbar in Word. Images of various metals could be paired with a drop-down form field from which children select the correct metal. This sort of approach allows children to concentrate on getting the answer right, without the pressure of having to remember how to spell a difficult word. Hard-to-explain concepts such as solids in science can be taught more memorably through a presentation showing solids, liquids and gases. Likewise, an Internet animation demonstrating the movement of blood around the body can speed up the learning process and put things into the correct context.

Summarising

Jenny Y7 Down's Syndrome

Jenny is good at reading and writing but her work is sometimes unimaginative and pedestrian. She has problems concentrating if there is lots of detail. Her SENCO has taught her to use the Autosummarise tool on Word which picks out the main points for her. Here is an example:

William Wilberforce (1759–1833), born in Hull, educated at the University of Cambridge. He became Member of Parliament for Hull in 1780 at the age of 21. He worked closely with the Prime Minister William Pitt and in 1785 started his campaign against the slave trade.

At that time African people were taken on British slave ships to the Caribbean Islands to grow tobacco and sugar. Many British ship owners, merchants and landowners made big profits from the trade. Wilberforce had joined the Evangelical Church in 1784 and in 1823 was one of the first to join the Anti-Slavery Society. Wilberforce gathered evidence about the conditions on the ships. The descriptions he wrote shocked people and gradually more and more joined his campaign. In 1807 Parliament made it illegal to trade in slaves. He then worked to abolish slavery and campaigned for over 25 years with the Anti-Slavery Society. Because of poor health, he had to retire from Parliament in 1825.

Parliament agreed in 1833 to give freedom to all slaves in British lands and to compensate the slave owners. Wilberforce heard the news just a few days before he died and said, 'Thank God that I should live to witness a day in which England is willing to give twenty million pounds for the Abolition of slavery'.

Images

Images might include digital photographs or video clips, scanned images, animations, clip art or Internet images. Conventional film photographs can be scanned into a computer and used in the same way as a digital photograph, but this is not as immediate. We can go back over the images and, through individual work and discussion, make sure vocabulary has been assimilated and that children have grasped concepts.

Still images can be used to record processes such as bread-making, provide visual timetables, support vocabulary, spelling and grammar and act as visual clues for writing across the curriculum. A series of photos of a familiar toy can teach prepositions in French: 'le chien est devant le placard; . . . sous la table, . . . dans la pantoufle, . . . derrière le livre.' It can be printed out, or used on screen, where children see the image and predict the text that will appear on a mouse click, using the animation feature.

Many children benefit from re-living an event in order to assimilate the experience, reflect upon it and develop the language to talk about it. The digital camera means pupils can collect a series of images that can be quickly transferred to a computer and displayed on screen or printed out. This helps them to develop the ability to recall and recount, to interact with others and develop their communication skills alongside their general understanding.

Matthew Y9 Cognitive and learning difficulties

Matthew is a very passive boy. He has no curiosity, no strong likes or dislikes. He has problems with most humanities subjects because he has no empathy and no real sense of what is required. When the class went to visit a museum for their work on the Civil War, he was completely unmoved. To him, it was just another building and he could not really link it with the work they had done in history.

With digital photography, Matthew would have to make decisions about what pictures to take. He would be able to use them as visual stimulus, develop his visual memory and link what he was reading about the Civil War to real objects he had seen.

(Read more about Matthew in Appendix 3.)

Digital video

Digital video is certainly opening up new opportunities for teaching, learning, and recording pupil progress and achievement. Video clips and the use of web cams can bring learning alive. Projection on a screen or whiteboard can make things larger and more accessible than in the real world. Watch a snail moving, magnified on a whiteboard, look at the swirls on the shell, write up children's comments on the board as they watch. Digital video cameras are not difficult to use and Windows XP Moviemaker or Apple iMovie allow for easy editing. You can add some text and a good quality sound file so pupils can hear words and sounds.

Children generally will learn the skills needed to present their own ideas and to respond to the demands of school in new and exciting ways. One girl working on the Exxon Valdez oil spill researched it on the Web, producing a series of bullet-pointed slides with images. She used the animation facility which meant that she could control when images and text appeared on screen at the touch of a mouse or switch. This was an exciting, creative homework, and a resource which could be used with other classes – you wouldn't get so much value out of an essay!

References

[1] DfES (2003) *Fulfilling the potential.* London: HMSO 0265/2003.

[2] Ofsted (2002) *ICT in schools: Effect of government initiatives.* London: HMSO.

[3] http://www.ictadvice.org.uk/downloads/guidance_doc/ictcoordsecondary_guide.doc

[4] This extract comes from *Transforming the Way we Learn – A Vision for the Future* of *ICT in Schools.* The full text of this document is available at: http://www.dfes.gov.uk/ictfutures

Appendices

SEN and Disability Act 2001 (SENDA)

INSET activity

1 The SEN and Disability Act 2001 amends the Disability Discrimination Act 1995 to include schools' and LEAs' responsibility to provide for pupils and students with disabilities.

2 The definition of a disability in this Act is:

'someone who has a physical or mental impairment that has an effect on his or her ability to carry out normal day-to-day activities. The effect must be:

- substantial (that is more than minor or trivial); and
- long term (that is, has lasted or is likely to last for at least a year or for the rest of the life of the person affected); and
- adverse'

Activity: List any pupils that you come across that would fall into this category.

3 The Act states that the responsible body for a school must take such steps as it is reasonable to take to ensure that disabled pupils and disabled prospective pupils are not placed at substantial disadvantage in comparison with those who are not disabled.

Activity: Give an example of something which might be considered 'a substantial disadvantage'.

4 The duty on the school to make reasonable adjustments is anticipatory. This means that a school should not wait until a disabled pupil seeks admission to consider what adjustments it might make generally to meet the needs of disabled pupils.

Activity: Think of two reasonable adjustments that could be made in your school/department.

5 The school has a duty to plan strategically for increasing access to the school education. This includes provision of information for pupils and parents (e.g. Braille or taped versions of brochures), improving the physical environment for disabled students and increasing access to the curriculum by further differentiation.

Activity: Consider ways of increasing access to the school for a pupil requesting admission who has Down's Syndrome with low levels of literacy and a heart condition that affects strenuous physical activity.

6 Schools need to be proactive in seeking out information about a pupil's disability (by establishing good relationships with parents and carers, asking about disabilities during admission interviews, etc.) and ensuring that all staff who might come across the pupil are aware of the pupil's disability.

Activity: List the opportunities that occur in your school for staff to gain information about disabled students. How can these be improved on?

What do we really think?

INSET activity

Each member of the department should choose two of these statements and pin them up on the noticeboard for an overview of staff opinion. The person leading the session (Head of Department, SENCO, senior manager) should be ready to address any negative feedback and take forward the department in a positive approach.

Children with more severe problems will get no benefit from studying ICT and will just hold other children back.

Statemented children are the SENCO's responsibility and should be concentrating on basic skills instead of learning about technology.

Word processing is great for every pupil. We can devise a lot of activities that are not reliant on good reading and writing skills.

Some pupils are only interested in playing games and there's no point in teaching them anything else.

I want to be able to cater for pupils with SEN and would find it beneficial to work with an expert in SEN.

PowerPoint opens up new worlds, especially for pupils who have limited language or sensory impairments.

If their behaviour distracts other pupils in any way, youngsters with SEN should be withdrawn from the class.

Pupils with special needs have the right to use a computer. They will need to use word processing and email to communicate with the world.

Children need to learn about ICT. It's the new basic skill and it's everywhere from cash points to supermarkets.

I need much more time to plan if pupils with SEN are going to be coming to my lessons.

I have enough to do working out the strategy for ICT without worrying about pupils who can barely read or write.

This is a photocopiable exercise.

A sample ICT policy

Date: _____

Review date: _____

The policy was developed by SMT, the ICT Co-ordinator, and the ICT Working Group and is subject to an eighteen month review.

This policy provides a structured framework to reflect upon and improve present curricular practice and administrative management, and will provide the basis for future planning. It will:

- reflect the aims and values of the school

- define the contribution that ICT makes to pupils' learning

- describe how ICT is used on a day-to-day basis

Access to ICT is a fundamental entitlement. The school provides facilities for whole-class work. There are also smaller specialist areas for science, technology and MFL. An on-line booking system operates for all ICT resources. There is Internet access and the school has developed its own intranet facility. The school has computers for individual use for both students and staff to borrow. All staff and students have access to e-mail and can access this from any networked machines.

ICT has a vital role to play in:

- improving still further the quality of teaching and learning

- supporting good teaching practice

- motivating staff and pupils

- fulfilling National Curriculum requirements

- providing effective and efficient information systems

- providing access to resources

Key factors which will influence developments:

- funding

- technological developments

- ICT initiatives

- Continuing Professional Development for all staff

- the level of pupils' ICT skills

Anticipated outcomes include:

- an increased use of ICT in lessons
- development of teaching and learning strategies
- improved staff awareness and use of ICT in lessons
- improved staff awareness of the value of ICT for administration
- improved school management information systems
- creation and sharing of resources

Roles and responsibilities

The ICT Development Team consists of a deputy head, an ICT co-ordinator and an ICT system manager. This team will audit current provision and practice, identify and prioritise needs, and develop, implement and evaluate policies. All staff, including support staff, will be encouraged to contribute to the process.

Curriculum organisation

ICT is taught as a discrete subject to all pupils at Key Stage 3.

ICT is a discrete subject within Key Stage 4. Pupils may be entered for GNVQ Full Intermediate ICT, Key Skills Level 2 or GCSE ICT.

ICT is integrated into departmental policies. Members of the ICT Development Team provide guidance to other staff, helping them to develop schemes of work, highlight ICT provision. Schemes of work are reviewed on an annual basis with a monitoring provision throughout the year.

Equal Opportunities

All pupils, regardless of ability, are provided with opportunities to use ICT within individual programmes. Pupils are assessed, their needs identified and suitable ICT activities are put in place. In some cases they will work in small groups with Teaching Assistants (TAs).

There will be a mixture of teacher-centred and student-centred approaches, individual and group work. There will be an emphasis on problem solving, creativity and research.

Awareness training on accessibility issues should be built into the general ICT training programme. All staff need to be aware that some pupils will benefit from the use of specialist access equipment such as roller-balls or keyboard guards. Staff should also be aware that tailored computer accessibility profiles will be a great help to many pupils. This could provide them with their preferred font size, background and text colour and mouse speed, and will make the user interface more friendly.

A clear procedure should be in place for the assessment of an individual pupil's accessibility needs and the practical implementation of profiles and equipment installation. Subject teachers and specialist support workers should discuss with the pupil their preferred computer configuration and suggest possible equipment to improve accessibility. When this has been tried and tested, a request should go to the ICT System Manager or Technician for the required equipment or profile to be set up on the network.

Technical support

Technical support is provided by the ICT System Manager and technician, although outside help is called for when required. When technical problems occur, these should be reported to the System Manager and entered into the Computer Book.

Training

It is a priority to upgrade staff ICT skills. Every member of staff should complete a skills' audit to highlight particular needs. The ICT Development Team will consider ways of meeting these needs. This might range from peer support to external training courses. The school is committed to a continuous process of INSET.

Resources

Software needs are identified by subject staff. As well as generic packages, (word processing, databases, spreadsheets, etc), subject staff should be encouraged to identify specific software including CD-ROMs, games and simulations for their curriculum area.

Security

All machines are housed within secure units and carry indelible marks to meet insurance requirements. All equipment comes under the terms of the school's insurance policy. Windows, doors and fittings all meet security standards.

Health and safety

The department has adopted the LEA and school Health and Safety policies.

Management Information System

The Management Information System is constantly reviewed. Training is provided by external agencies when required. Appropriate levels of security are provided to satisfy the requirements of the Data Protection Act and the Misuse of Computer Act.

Assessing, Recording and Reporting

Methods of assessment are under continuous review to ensure appropriate differentiation and progression. They may include teacher observation, group work, homework assignments and course work. Where pupils would benefit from specialist software or hardware in order to access the curriculum, this will be provided.

Students' work is marked and moderated regularly in line with the school's marking policy, with levels awarded based on the National Curriculum or GCSE criteria. Teacher assessment is an integral part of the assessment process. A range of assignments will be provided to stretch the most able whilst allowing all pupils to show what they can achieve.

Grades are recorded and are used for reporting purposes, for planning new work and as guidance to new staff. Key Stage 3 work is stored until the student leaves school. Examination work is stored in accordance with examination board requirements. All students' work is stored in electronic format, backed up to CD-ROM.

Future developments

An open learning centre is being developed. This will give access to the Internet and intranet to support the delivery of the curriculum.

All Internet use is supervised. Pupils must sign a copy of the Acceptable Use Policy before they are provided with usernames and passwords to give them access to the Internet and intranet. The rules are shown on posters in the ICT rooms and in letters to parents. The school's policies regarding Internet use are regularly updated in line with recommendations from outside agencies.

Sample policy based on statements in Chapter 2

Example: All members of the department will ensure that the needs of all pupils with SEN are met, according to the aims of the school and its SEN policy.

Example: The member of staff with responsibility for overseeing the provision of SEN within the department will attend liaison meetings and feed back to other members of the department. He will maintain the department's SEN information file, attend appropriate training and disseminate this to all departmental staff. All information will be treated with confidentiality.

Example: The pupils are grouped according to ability as informed by Key Stage 2 results, reading scores and any other relevant performance or social information.

Example: It is understood that pupils with SEN may receive additional support if they have a statement of SEN, are at School Action Plus or School Action. The staff in the ICT department will aim to support the pupils to achieve their targets as specified on their IEPs and will provide feedback for IEP or statement reviews. Pupils with SEN will be included in the departmental monitoring system used for all pupils. Additional support will be requested as appropriate.

Example: The department will provide suitably differentiated materials and where appropriate, specialist resources for pupils with SEN. Additional texts are available for those pupils working below National Curriculum level 3. At Key Stage 4 an alternative course to GCSE is offered at Entry level but, where possible, pupils with SEN will be encouraged to reach their full potential and follow a GCSE course. Support staff will be provided with curriculum information in advance of lessons and will also be involved in lesson planning. A list of resources is available in the department handbook and on the noticeboard.

Example: A record of training undertaken, specialist skills and training required will be kept in the department handbook. Requests for training will be considered in line with the department and school improvement plan.

Example: The Department SEN policy will be monitored by the Head of Department on a planned annual basis, with advice being sought from the SENCO as part of a three-yearly review process.

Health and safety

Clear access is essential for pupils with mobility and visual challenges.

- Ensure doors open fully.

- Store coats and bags safely.

- Avoid trailing cables.

- Mark worktop corners and edges with bright tape.

- Avoid placing equipment on the floor or in unexpected places.

- If you are working with programmable toys, such as floor turtles, clearly define the working area and if possible cordon off the work space.

- Consider alternatives to floor turtles, such as the smaller toys that can be used on a table top inside a large tray, or computer software.

Ambient lighting and positioning of displays is crucial for pupils with visual challenges.

- Try to minimise reflected light on monitor screens.

- Ensure that pupils are in a position to see displays on the whiteboard.

- Consider using a web cam to project details of experiments or practical processes onto a whiteboard.

- Levels of lighting in ICT areas should be slightly lower than standard classrooms to give an appropriate contrast between screen and background.

- Use semi-translucent blinds in rooms where glare from the sun is a problem.

Awareness of the dangers of glare when using a data projector must be instilled in all pupils.

- Ensure that all SEN pupils understand this danger and are supervised when using an interactive whiteboard or when a data projector is in use.

- Becta advice states that pupils should never look directly into the beam of the projector.

- Ideally, pupils should keep their back towards the beam when working at an interactive whiteboard.

- You may consider using a neutral density filter to reduce the brightness of the beam when using an interactive whiteboard with pupils who are unable to appreciate the dangers.

- Careful positioning of the projector may reduce glare dangers. A ceiling-mounted projector is less likely to produce direct glare than a table-mounted one.

Ambient noise should be kept to a minimum for pupils with hearing impairments.

- When purchasing equipment such as data projectors and fans, check their operating noise level in the specifications.

- If possible choose computers with low noise level cooling fans.

- Encourage the use of personal headphones to avoid distracting noise from CD-ROMs.

Consider carefully the positioning of interactive whiteboards for pupils with mobility challenges.

- Ideally, whiteboards should be positioned so all pupils can reach them, but often a compromise has to be made between the best height for access and the height that affords all pupils a good view.

- A wireless keyboard and mouse may give a wheelchair user the opportunity to contribute to interactive whiteboard sessions.

- A wireless graphics pad may be another solution.

(For further advice and information on health and safety issues related to ICT and education visit the Becta ICT advice site.)

Keeping strategies in mind

Instructions for INSET activity

This activity should only take about ten minutes but can be used for additional discussion on strategies, concentrating on the easy ones to implement or the ones already being used.

1 Photocopy onto paper or card.

2 Cut the first column off the sheet.

3 Cut out the remaining boxes.

4 Either keep the two sets of boxes separate, firstly matching the characteristics, then the strategies, or use all together.

Alternative activity: make the boxes bigger with room for additional strategies, or remove a couple of the strategies so staff can add any they have used or can identify.

Special Educational Need	Characteristics	Strategies
Attention Deficit Disorder- with or without hyperactivity	• has difficulty following instructions and completing tasks • easily distracted by noise, movement of others, objects attracting attention • can't stop talking, interrupts others, calls out • acts impulsively without thinking about the consequences	• keep instructions simple – the one sentence rule • make eye contact and use the pupil's name when speaking to him • sit the pupil away from obvious distractions • provide clear routines and rules, rehearse them regularly
Autistic Spectrum Disorder	• may experience high levels of stress and anxiety when routines are changed • may have a literal understanding of language • more often interested in objects rather than people • may be sensitive to light, sound, touch or smell	• give a timetable for each day • warn the pupil about changes to usual routine • avoid using too much eye contact as it can cause distress • use simple clear language, avoid using metaphor, sarcasm
Down's Syndrome	• takes longer to learn and consolidate new skills • limited concentration • has difficulties with thinking, reasoning, sequencing • has better social than academic skills • may have some sight, hearing, respiratory and heart problems	• use simple, familiar language • give time for information to be processed • break lesson up into a series of shorter, varied tasks • accept a variety of ways of recording work: drawings, diagrams, photos, video
Hearing impairment	• may be mild, moderate or severe • may be monoaural, conductive, sensory or mixed loss	• check on the best seating position • check that the pupil can see your face for expressions and lip reading • indicate where a pupil is speaking from during class discussion; only allow one speaker at a time
Dyscalculia	• has a discrepancy between development level and general ability in maths • has difficulty counting by rote • misses out or reverses numbers • has difficulty with directions, left and right • losing track of turns in games, dance	• provide visual aids, number lines, lists of rules, formulae, words • encourage working out on paper • provide practical objects to aid learning

Case studies

Read the case studies which follow. There are suggestions for classroom strategies here but there is also space for you to add your own.

Kuli (male) Y8, Hearing impairment

Kuli has profound hearing loss. He has some hearing in his right ear but is heavily reliant on visual cues ranging from lip reading to studying body language and facial expression to get the gist and tone of what people are saying. He often misses crucial details. Reading is a useful alternative input and his mechanical reading skills are good but he does not always get the full message because of language delay. He has problems with new vocabulary and with asking and responding to questions.

He follows the same timetable as the rest of his class for most of the week but he has some individual tutorial sessions with a teacher of the deaf to help with his understanding of the curriculum and to focus on his speech and language development. This is essential, but it does mean that he misses some classes so he is not always 'up to speed' with a subject.

He has a good sense of humour, but appreciates visual jokes, more than ones which are language based. He is very literal and is puzzled by all sorts of idioms. He was shocked when he heard that someone had been 'painting the town red' as he thought this was an act of vandalism! Even when he knows what he wants to say, he does not always have the words or structures to communicate accurately what he knows.

Everyone is very pleasant and quite friendly to him, but he is not really part of any group and quite often misunderstands what other students are saying. He has a Learning Assistant which, again, marks him out as different. He gets quite frustrated because he always has ideas that are too complex for his expressive ability. He can be very sulky and has temper tantrums.

Strategies

- A word grid with key vocabulary will help with composition and also can be printed out and used as a vocabulary and concept list outside the classroom.

- Try to establish that TAs using Sign Supported English consistently use the same signs for terminology.

- ....

- ....

Bhavini (female) Y9, Visual impairment

Bhavini has very little useful sight. She uses a stick to get around the large comprehensive school where she is a pupil and some of the other children make cruel comments about this which she finds very hurtful. She also wears glasses with thick lenses which she hates. On more than one occasion, she has been knocked over in the corridor but she insists that these incidents were accidents and that she is not being bullied. However, her sight is so poor that she could not recognise anyone who picked on her.

She has a certain amount of specialist equipment such as talking scales in cookery and a CCTV for textbooks, and is always conscious of being different. Her classmates accept her but she is very cut off as she does not make eye contact or see well enough to find people she knows to sit with at break. She spends a lot of time hanging around the support area. Her form tutor has tried to get other children to take her under their wing or to escort her to Humanities, which is in another building, but this has bred resentment. She has friends outside school at the local Phab club and has taken part in regional VI Athletics tournaments, but she opts out of sport at school if she can. Some of the teachers are concerned about Health and Safety issues and there has been talk about her being disapplied from science.

She has a reading age approximately three years behind her chronological age and spells phonetically. Many of the teaching strategies which are used to make learning more interesting disadvantage her. The lively layout of her French book with cartoons and speech bubbles is a nightmare. Even if she has a page on her CCTV or has a photocopy of the text enlarged she cannot track which bit goes where. At the end of one term she turned up at the support base asking for some work to do because, 'They're all watching videos.'

Strategies

- Bhavini needs to improve her keyboard skills and would benefit from a touch-typing course. She could practise this in homework club and at home, as well as having some sessions during the school week.

- She may need extra support with any form of control technology project. When others are impressed that a machine works, doors open or a turtle moves, she may not be able to see it. She may need a session where she touches something and feels the effect of programming in instructions.

- ....

- ....

Megan Y10, Wheelchair user

Nicknamed Little Miss Angry, everyone knows when Megan is around! She is very outgoing, loud and tough. No one feels sorry for her – they wouldn't dare! Megan has spina bifida and needs personal care as well as educational support. She has upset a number of the less experienced Classroom Assistants who find her a real pain. Some of the teachers like her because she is very sparky. If she likes a subject, she works hard – or at least she did until this year.

Megan has to be up very early for her parents to help get her ready for school before the bus comes at 7.50 a.m. She lives out of town and is one of the first to be picked up and one of the last to be dropped off, so she has a longer school day than many of her classmates. Tiredness can be a problem as everything takes her so long to do and involves so much effort. Now she is 15 she has started working towards her GCSEs and has the potential to get several A to Cs particularly in maths and sciences. She is intelligent, but is in danger of becoming disaffected because everything is so much harder for her than for other children. Recently she has lost her temper with a teacher, made cruel remarks to a very sensitive child and turned her wheelchair round so she was sitting with her back to a supply teacher. She has done no homework for the last few weeks saying that she doesn't see the point as 'no one takes a crip seriously.'

Strategies

- Explore the use of voice recognition software to enable Megan to be more independent. Hopefully she will find she is able to do more work before becoming too tired and this will encourage and motivate her to keep going.

- Predictive word processing is another option to improve her work rate and output of text.

- Some schools use a series of stickers with faces to indicate emotions. These can be put on the monitor to show, for example – 'I don't want to talk right now', or 'I'm fed up', or 'I am tired'. Teachers and TAs can see her mood before risking confrontation.

- ....

- ....

Steven Y8, BESD

'Stevie' is a real charmer – sometimes! He is totally inconsistent: one day, he is full of enthusiasm; the next day, he is very tricky and he needs to be kept on target. He thrives on attention. In primary school, he spent a lot of time sitting by the teacher's desk and seemed to enjoy feeling special. If he sat there he would get on with his work, but then as soon as he moved to sit with his friends he wanted to make sure he was the centre of attention.

Steven sometimes seems lazy, looking for the easy way out, but at other times he is quite dynamic and has lots of bright ideas. He can't work independently and has a very short attention span. No one has very high expectations of him and he is not about to prove them wrong.

Some of the children don't like him because he can be a bully but really he is not nasty. He is a permanent lieutenant for some of the tougher boys and does things to win their approval.

He is a thief, but mostly he takes silly things, designed to annoy rather than for any monetary value. He was found with someone's library ticket and stole one shoe from the changing rooms during PE.

Since his mother has taken up with a new partner, there has been a deterioration in behaviour and Steven has also been cautioned by police after stealing from a local DIY store. He has just been suspended for throwing a chair at a teacher, but staff suspect, that this was because he was on a dare. He certainly knows how to get attention.

Strategies

- Steven needs to improve his self-image. He may respond to the digital cameras, scanners and other multimedia peripherals more than to word processing or spreadsheets.

- Encourage Steven to save his work regularly as he may only work in short spurts. Time him and prove to him that he is staying on task longer.

- ....

- ....

Matthew Y9, Cognitive and learning difficulties

Matthew is a very passive boy. He has no curiosity, no strong likes or dislikes. One teacher said, 'He's the sort of boy who says yes to everything to avoid further discussion, but I sometimes wonder if he understands anything.'

He is quite a loner. He knows all the children and does not feel uncomfortable with them but is always on the margins. Often in class he sits and does nothing, just stares into space. He is no trouble and, indeed, if there is any kind of conflict, he absents himself or ignores it. No one knows very much about him as he never volunteers any information. In French, he once said that he had a dog and one teacher has seen him on the local common with a terrier, but no one is sure if it was his.

He does every piece of work as quickly as possible to get it over with. His work is messy and there is no substance to anything he does, which makes it hard for teachers to suggest a way forward, or indeed to find anything to praise. Matthew often looks a bit grubby and is usually untidy. He can be quite clumsy and loses things regularly but does not bother to look for them. He does less than the minimum.

He is in a low set for maths but stays in the middle. He has problems with most humanities subjects because he has no empathy and no real sense of what is required. When the class went to visit a museum for their work on the Civil War, he was completely unmoved. To him, it was just another building, and he could not really link it with the work they had done in history.

Strategies

- Clicker grids with key words and topic vocabulary can help, not just with spelling and composition but also with the concepts involved in ICT.

- ICT will improve the appearance of Matthew's work. Encourage him to surf the Internet to find out about topics. Show him how to use the Images option of Google and find pictures to illustrate his work.

- ....

- ....

Susan Y10, complex difficulties: ASD

Susan is a tall, very attractive girl who has been variously labelled as having Asperger's and 'cocktail party syndrome'. She talks fluently but usually about something totally irrelevant. She is very charming and her language is sometimes quite sophisticated, but her understanding and ability to use language for school work operate at a much lower level. Her reading is excellent on some levels but she cannot draw inferences from the printed word. If you ask her questions about what she has read, she looks blank, echoes what you have said, looks puzzled or changes the subject – something she is very good at.

She finds relationships quite difficult. She is very popular, especially with the boys in her class. They think she is a laugh. There have been one or two problems with older boys in the school. Her habit of standing too close to people and her over-familiarity in manner have led to misunderstandings which have upset her badly. Her best friend Laura is very protective of her and tries to mother her, to the extent of doing some of her work for her so she won't get into trouble.

Her work is limited. In art all her pictures look the same, very small, cramped drawings, and she does not like to use paint because, 'it's messy.' She finds it very hard to relate to the wider world and sees everything in terms of her own experience. The class has been studying *Macbeth* and she has not moved beyond saying, 'I don't believe in witches and ghosts'.

Some teachers think she is being wilfully stupid or not paying attention. She seems to be attention seeking as she is very poor at turn taking, and shouts out in class if she thinks of something to say or wants to know how to spell a word. When she was younger, she used to retreat under the desk when she was upset and had to be coaxed out. She is still easily offended and cannot bear being teased. She has an answer for everything and, while it may not be sensible or reasonable, there is an underlying logic.

Strategies

- Keep activities very simple to start with. Encourage her to develop presentation skills in *Word* and *PowerPoint*.

- Get her working with different people in each lesson until you find pairings which work.

- Writing frames or grids to be filled in will give a structure to her work and stop her wandering off into irrelevancies.

- ....

- ....

Jenny Y7, Down's Syndrome

Jenny is a very confident child who has been cherished and encouraged by her mother and older brothers and sisters. She is very assertive and is more than capable of dealing with spiteful comments: 'I don't like it when you call me names. You're cruel and I hate you', but this assertiveness can lead to obstinacy. She is prone to telling teachers that they are wrong!

She is good at reading and writing but her work is sometimes unimaginative and pedestrian. She enjoys maths and biology but finds the rest of the science curriculum hard going. She has started to put on weight and tries to avoid PE. She has persuaded her mother to provide a note saying that she tires easily, but staff know that she is a bundle of energy and is an active member of an amateur theatre group which performs musicals. She has a good singing voice and enjoys dancing.

She went to a local nursery and primary school and fitted in well. She always had some one to sit next to and was invited to all the best birthday parties. Teachers and other parents frequently praised her and she felt special.

Now in secondary school, everything has changed. Some of her friends from primary school have made new friendships and don't want to spend so much time with her. She is very hurt by this and feels excluded. She is also struck by how glamorous some of the older girls look and this has made her more self-conscious.

Strategies

- Writing frames will give a structure to Jenny's work and may help her to work independently on certain topics.

- Explore the use of *Symbols* from Widgit. Encourage her to look at symbol-supported websites.

- Help her to develop skills with some of the fun elements of ICT – making posters, putting in borders, book marking her favourite sites on the Web.

- ....

- ....

Harry Y7, Dyslexia

Harry is a very anxious little boy and although he has now started at secondary school, he still seems to be a 'little boy'. His parents have been very concerned about his slow progress in reading and writing and arranged for a dyslexia assessment when he was eight years old. They also employ a private tutor who comes to the house for two hours per week, and they spend time each evening and at weekends hearing him read and working on phonics with him.

Harry expresses himself well orally, using words which are very sophisticated and adult. His reading is improving (RA 8.4) but his handwriting and spelling are so poor that it is sometimes difficult to work out what he has written. He doesn't just confuse *b* and *d* but also *h* and *y*, *p* and *b*. Increasingly he uses a small bank of words that he knows he can spell.

His parents want him to be withdrawn from French on the grounds that he has enough problems with English. The French teacher reports that Harry is doing well with his comprehension and spoken French and is one of the more able children in the class.

Some staff get exasperated with Harry as he is quite clumsy, seems to be in a dream half the time and cannot remember a simple sequence of instructions. He has difficulty telling left from right and so is often talking about the wrong diagram in a book or is out of step in dance classes. 'He's just not trying,' said one teacher, while others think he needs 'to grow up a bit.'

He is popular with the girls in his class and recently has made friends with some of the boys in the choir. Music is Harry's great passion but his parents are not willing for him to learn an instrument at the moment.

Strategies

- Teach Harry to touch-type as this will help him to develop a kinaesthetic approach to spelling and long term will relieve pressure on memory.

- Teach him how to use the spell checker.

- Investigate a program such as *TextHelp Read and Write* which has a dyslexia-friendly spell checker and a prediction window, and will read back text. It sits on top of *Word* so Harry would still be using the same software as everyone else.

- ....

- ....

Computer Accessibility

The mouse

Clumsy children – whether with special needs or not – find it hard to double click to open a folder or file. Slow down the mouse speed and they will soon get the hang of it. But there are also other things you can do.

Some pupils, especially those who have limited movement in their hands, have difficulty using a mouse because it requires some dexterity. If they can operate a keyboard effectively, try MouseKeys which turns the numeric keypad into an alternative mouse, can move the mouse pointer around the screen, and click the buttons.

Go to Start – Control Panel – Accessibility Options – Mouse

MouseKeys is usually slower than using a mouse but it can provide a straightforward way to control the mouse pointer.

There are alternatives for pupils who are not able to double click or highlight text. Click at the beginning of the text you want to select, hold down the shift key and then click at the end of the extract. Your chosen text will now be highlighted. If that doesn't work, a facility called
Click lock can be highly recommended:

1 Go to Start – Control Panel – Mouse – Buttons

2 Click on the little check box to turn on click lock.

3 Find a piece of text.

4 Click your mouse and keep it still for a few seconds.

5 Now go to the end of the extract, click and hold again.

6 Did it seem slow? Then open up the settings box in the click lock option and change the timings. Try again.

Pointers

Let's look at pointers next. The Pointers tab lets you define the size and shape of the Windows pointer. Some people will find it easier to spot a big pointer on screen. The speed that the pointer moves, in response to the movement of the mouse, is set by Pointer Speed. If you have difficulty controlling the mouse pointer accurately, try slowing the speed down. Pointer Trails leave a 'trail' behind the pointer as it moves, so it can make the pointer more visible. This is worth checking, especially with learners with dyslexia.

1 Go to Start – Control Panel – Mouse – Pointers

2 Experiment!

Keyboard

Perhaps some of your pupils have poor motor control and hit two keys at once or get a string of repeated letters. Some pupils just cannot hold down two or three keys at the same time so Ctrl, Alt, Del is impossible.

Using Sticky Keys will affect the three functions of the Control, Alt and Shift keys, which are called 'modifiers' because they modify whatever key you hit next, turning it into a capital letter or a command. You need either to latch or to lock Sticky Keys.

---

1 Go to Start – Control Panel – Accessibility Options – keyboard

2 Look at the Sticky Keys option and make sure there is a little tick in the check box.

3 Click on Settings.

4 Make sure there is a tick in every box to activate all settings.

5 Open a word-processing document.

6 Activate the Sticky Keys option by hitting the shift key five times.

7 Press Shift.

8 Press the £ sign.

9 You will now see a pound sign, but everything else you type will be in lower case. You have LATCHED the sticky keys. This means you have snapped shift on and off.

StickyKeys

But what if you want to type a whole series of keys? If the Sticky Keys function is active, you can lock the modifier by pressing it twice. If the Sticky Keys sound features are enabled, you will hear a short double-note beep after the first tap and a single high beep after the second tap. Once a modifier key is locked, it stays locked until it is pressed a third time; it will then keep working until you press it again. So if you hit Shift twice you will type in capital letters until you press it again. In practice, not many people use the lock feature because there are often alternatives such as the Caps Lock button.

Go to Start – Control Panel – keyboard

You have three options here: repeat delay, repeat rate, and cursor blink rate. If you have difficulty taking your finger off the key quickly, and tend to type extra letters by mistake, try using a longer Repeat Delay.

Alternatively, choose Slow down keyboard repeat rate. Change the timing to one second and try it out in the test area. You should find you cannot repeat the same letter unless you wait for a second. Choosing Repeat Delay slows down the first repeated letter. Choosing Repeat Rate slows down all repeats after the first one.

User profiles

If the computer is going to be used by several people, you may want to have particular settings for individuals. For example, Bhavini needs a large mouse pointer which leaves trails across the screen, while Kim has photophobia and needs a dark background with white writing, to reduce the brightness on the screen and to change the colour of the cursor to make it easier to see.

You can save all these settings as a User Profile from the Passwords Control Panel. The User Profile can also start up with different programs or folders on the desktop for a particular user or group of users. For example, Wendy has autism and is resistant to change. She needs her desktop to look exactly the same each time she logs on.

The settings can also include different Start menus and program groups. This might be useful in a setting where you want to restrict access to particular Start menu items like the Control Panels.

When the computer starts up, it asks you to type in your name, and a password if you wish. Then it loads the accessibility options you have created.

Think about it

What are the key points for and against User Profiles?

What will be your policy in your school?

How will you justify it to critics?

Shortcut commands

Some people like using program menus while others use the icons. However, many experienced users find that there are lots of shortcuts using the Control or Shift keys and different letters of the alphabet. Want to write some fractions or put in a number squared? It is fiddly to do this through the font menu but highlight the number and use the Control = command and you will get a quick result.

There are many commands and shortcuts but the following are the most common and most useful:

General commands

Save	Ctrl S	
Find	Ctrl F	
Hyperlink	Ctrl K	Switches on or off
New document	Ctrl N	
Open document	Ctrl O	
Close document	Ctrl W	
Select all	Ctrl A	
Help	F1	

Working with text

Font	Ctrl D	
Superscript	Shift Control =	Useful for maths e.g. 5^2
Subscript	Ctrl =	Useful for maths e.g. $^{3/4}2_5$
Copy	Control C	
Cut	Control X	
Paste	Control V	
Undo	Control Z	
Print	Control P	
Bold	Ctrl + B	add/remove formatting
Italic	Ctrl + I	add/remove formatting
Underline	Ctrl + U	add/remove formatting
Change case	Shift F3	
Spellchecker	F7	
Thesaurus	Shift F7	
Single spacing	Control 1	Changes double to single spacing
Double spacing	Control 2	Changes single to double spacing

ICT Level Descriptors – Level 4

- You will need to show that you **understand** why it is **important** to take **care** when asking **questions** when trying to find things out.

- You need to show care when **collecting**, **finding** and **using** information.

- You need to show **clearly** that you **understand** that **poor quality information** will mean that your final piece of work will be **poor quality** too.

- You need to **add** to information which you find, and put **two** or **more** pieces of information **together** which you found in **different** places.

- You need to show that you **understand** that your work will need to look **different**, and **contain** different **information**, depending on **who** it is for.

- You need to **share** information with other people in **different** ways, using **email** sometimes.

- You need to use computer equipment to **control things** very **accurately**, and to **record** information using **sensors**, such as temperature for example.

- You need to use **computer models** to **explore** situations and make **predictions**; for example, using a model to find out whether something will work or not, or how much something might cost.

- You need to **compare** the way you do things on a **computer** at **school** with the way you do things on a computer **elsewhere**, such as at home.

'ICT NC Level Descriptions in Pupil Language' (Justin Arnold, Pindar School 23 Oct. 03)
See: http://tre.ngfl.gov.uk/uploads/materials/13184/ICT%20Level%20Descriptions.doc

Key vocabulary

This list is drawn from Appendix 2 of the *Framework for teaching ICT capability: Years 7, 8 and 9*. It represents the vocabulary that most pupils operating within the range of expectation for Key Stage 3 will have met in their ICT lessons by the end of Year 7. Schools using the supplementary materials for teaching ICT capability at and below level 3 may wish to consider the vocabulary list and use it to develop key vocabulary that reflects the words their pupils have met and will meet in their ICT lessons.

Finding things out

accuracy/accurate, AND, archives, average, bar chart, browse, chart, classify, compact disc (CD) read-only memory (CD-ROM), computer, conclusion, content, contents list, copyright, data, data collection sheet, data handling, data structure, data type, database, desktop computer, dial up, disk drive, download, experiment, enquiry, field, file, file extension, file name, find, floppy disk, folder, frequency, graph, hardware, home page, hypothesis, identify, index, information, information source, Internet, intranet, key word, keyboard, laptop, load, locate/location, log on/log off, network, numeric, opinion/opinion poll, OR, origin/originator, password, pie chart, query, questionnaire, range, record, reliable/unreliable, report, represent, representation, save, search, search engine, search method, server, shared area, software, sort, survey, table, tally, uniform resource locator (URL), verify, viewpoint, web browser, web page, website, World Wide Web (WWW)

Developing ideas and making things happen

analogue, automate/automatic, calculate/calculation, cell, cell reference, column, control, control loop, digital, enter, flow chart, formula, formulae, gridlines, input, input device, label, logo, model, output, output device, pattern, predict, prediction, procedure, print area, probe, process, program, random number, relationship, repeat, repeated process, replicate, robot, row, rule, sensor, sequence of instructions, simulate/simulation, spreadsheet, store, switch, subtask, system, template, variable
Key Stage 3 Materials for teaching ICT capability at and below level 3 – Guide for senior leaders and subject leaders DfES 0382–2004.

Exchanging and sharing information

acknowledgement, address book/list, animate, atmosphere, attribute, audience, audio cassette recorder, bitmapped graphic/image, body text, bold, bullet points, capital letters, capture, clip art, colour scheme, copy, copyright, corporate image, crop, cursor, cut, delete, design brief, desktop publishing (DTP), digital camera, digital video disk (DVD), digital video software, display, document, drag, drop-down menu, duplicate, earphone, e-mail, effect, export, font, font size, footer, format, graphic(s), header, heading, hypertext, illustration, image, import, intended audience, italic, label, landscape, layer objects, layout, link, logo, manipulate, microphone, mouse, moving image, multimedia authoring, multimedia presentation, network, object(s), onscreen viewing, paint and draw software, paste, photograph, points, portrait, presentation software, projector/projection, print/printer, readability, resize, scale, scanner, screen, scroll/scroll bar, serif/ sans serif, shared area, slide show, slide view, sound, speaker, still image, storyboard/storyboarding, structure, style, subheading, Teletext, television (TV), text, transfer, typeface, underline, upper/lower case, vector graphic/image, video cassette recorder (VCR), video clip, voiceover, web publishing, white space, word processor

Reviewing, modifying and evaluating work as it progresses

adapt, annotate, assess/assessment, backup, check, clarity, criterion/criteria, criticise, develop, draft, edit, effective, efficient/efficiency, enhance, evaluate, evaluation, expected outcome, feature, fitness for purpose, improve, judge, organise, plan, produce, purpose, refine, review, revise, spell-check, test, value

Working with Teaching Assistants

- What will you expect from the Learning Assistant?
- Do all the ICT staff have a clear understanding of the roles and responsibilities of the LSA?
- What can they reasonably ask an LSA to do?
- Will he/she be expected to work with groups or individuals?
- What will be the status of the Teaching Assistant?
- How are Teaching Assistants referred to?
- Are pupils expected to treat them with the same degree of respect as they would a teacher?
- Should TAs suggest and make additional materials?
- Are LSAs responsible for care needs?
- Will the LSA be involved in planning?
- How will he/she feed back information about pupils' progress?
- Does he/she understand the importance of confidentiality?
- Will there be regular meetings between the HoD and LSA?
- Will they be expected to attend staff meetings?
- Should they provide written notes which could be incorporated into an IEP?
- Are LSAs responsible for setting up computers and finding other specialist equipment?
- Will opportunities be provided for him/her to become familiar with the hardware, software and teaching needs?
- Will training be available?
- Will support materials be provided?
- Will there be regular meetings?
- Will they be involved in review meetings with parents, other professionals, the child?

Acceptable use policy

Here is a sample policy for you to adapt to your own purposes:

Usernames and password

- You will be given a username and password.

- You will need this to use the network.

- You must keep the username and password private at all times.

- If you suspect that another pupil knows your password, you must report it immediately to ——————————————— (insert name and position).

- You must not try to logon with a username or password that is not yours.

Health and safety

- If you find any of the equipment does not work (e.g. flickering VDU displays, 'sticky' mice, etc.) report it to the teacher in charge.

- Do not move any ICT equipment, except to adjust angle of VDU, chair height, etc.

- Do not bring any food or drink into the ICT room.

- Do not disconnect or adjust any cabling.

- Behave responsibly while you are near ICT equipment. Any behaviour which may result in injury or damage is not allowed.

- Do not leave bags and other bulky items in gangways.

- If you are not sure where to store your items, ask the teacher in charge.

Disks and other media

- Do not bring any CDs, diskettes or other storage media into school without prior permission from a member of staff.

- All disks must be checked for viruses before being used on the network.

- Do not attempt to install or copy software on any computer without the express permission of ——————————————— (insert name and position).

- Any pupil found to be loading or using a disk or software will face disciplinary procedures.

Printing

- You will be allocated a set number of pages for printing per term.

- No more printing will be possible without permission from
  ———————————————— (insert name and position).

- If you print excessive amounts, you will be charged.

Using email in school

- Do not give out your home address or phone number or those of other students when using email.

- You must only give out your email address to people you know and trust.

- Report any email you receive from an unknown source.

- Using email for bullying is not acceptable.

- Any emails you send can be recorded and traced back to you.

Internet

- Your parent(s)/guardian(s) must have signed and returned a permission form before you can use the Internet.

- If you think anyone has been making unacceptable use of the Internet, report it at once to a member of staff.

- If you see any materials that are violent, dangerous, racist or contain inappropriate content, report them at once to a member of staff.

- If you are creating Web pages, these must be checked by a member of staff before being published on the Web.

- When copying materials from the Web, you will observe the laws of copyright. You must reference the sources used and state clearly the author.

- Remember that Internet access is monitored. Every time you visit – or try to visit – a site, it is recorded and can be traced back to you.

Sanctions

- You may be banned from using the Internet on a temporary or permanent basis.

- A letter will be sent to your parents telling them what you have done.

- There may be other sanctions and restrictions judged to be appropriate by the Head of Year/Head of Department.

Good examples of policies

'The Superhighway Safety' site has lots of information and some sample policies, forms and letters: http://safety.ngfl.gov.uk/schools/index.php3?S=2

King Edward VI School, Hampshire – rules for school use and for the after-school club: http://www.kes.hants.sch.uk/it/rules/

Trinity Church of England High School, Manchester – *a* list of rules which the pupil and parent/guardian must sign up to: http://www.trinityhigh.com/inform/aupinfo.htm

North Chadderton School, Oldham (Secondary) – an acceptable use policy for pupils and a separate policy for teachers: http://www.webschool.org.uk/aup.htm